CISTERCIAN FATHERS SERIES NUMBER FIVE

AELRED OF RIEVAULX

SPIRITUAL FRIENDSHIP

CISTERCIAN FATHERS SERIES NUMBER FIVE

AELRED OF RIEVAULX

Spiritual Friendship

Translated by
Mary Eugenia Laker SSND

Introduction by
Douglass Roby

CISTERCIAN PUBLICATIONS
Kalamazoo, Michigan
1977

Cistercian Fathers Series   ISBN 0-87907-000-5
The Works of Aelred of Rievaulx ISBN 0-87907-200-8
This volume   cloth   ISBN 0-87907-205-9
           paper   ISBN 0-87907-705-0

Library of Congress Catalog Card Number: 75-152480

Ecclesiastical permission to publish this book has been received from
Bernard Flanagan, Bishop of Worcester, July 13, 1970.

CONTENTS

INTRODUCTION

AELRED'S LIFE

THERE ARE SEVERAL REASONS why the life of Aelred should be briefly considered as an introduction to his *Spiritual Friendship*. In the first place it is clear that Aelred's early experiences had given him many of the raw materials from which he was later to build this uniquely moving dialogue. In the second place, the work itself contains a number of autobiographical reflections which become more meaningful when put in the context of what little we know of Aelred's background.

The north country, along the Anglo-Scottish border, had been a contested land and one rich in history for generations before Aelred's time. Part of the old Kingdom of Northumbria, brightly illuminated for us by the pen of Bede, it had suffered terribly at the hands of the Viking invaders from the beginning of the ninth century. The great monasteries and cathedral libraries had almost all vanished in smoke, and it was only with great effort and at the cost of much suffering that one of the great treasures of the country, the body of its patron St Cuthbert, had been preserved from the pillage.

As the smoke of the Viking invasions began to clear in the late tenth century, we catch our first glimpse of Aelred's family. His ancestors had the honorable position of treasurer of the shrine of St Cuthbert, whose bones had been carried from Lindisfarne to Chester-le-Street, and finally to Durham, where they found their lasting resting place in 995.[1] Aelred's

1. The best discussion of Aelred's ancestors is Aelred Squire, *Aelred of Rievaulx: a Study* (London, 1969), esp. pp. 5-11. Cited as *Aelred*.

great-grandfather personally tended the shrine, and seems not
to have offended the saint in any way by being a married
priest, producing a son Eilaf.

This Eilaf, Aelred's grandfather, inherited the living of
Hexham from his father, and proceded to pass it on to his
own son, another Eilaf. But the days of this comfortable
hereditary priesthood were doomed and the younger Eilaf
saw the end of such ancient Northumbrian customs. In Rome
the great reform movement which we associate with the name
of Pope Gregory VII was well underway, raising massive opposition in many lands from both the episcopate and the
princes. But in England, William the Conqueror found it very
much to his advantage to favor the pope's reform in return
for papal approval of his own conquest of the island. But in
spite of the almost super-human energy of William, and the
efforts of the new Norman aristocracy which soon occupied
the best lands and bishoprics of England, the customs of
centuries could not be wiped away overnight.[2]

Eilaf did find himself in a difficult position, however. Leaving his prebend at St Cuthbert's shrine in Durham, he retired
to live at Hexham in 1083 when the Norman bishop, William of
St Carilef, installed monks in the place of the cathedral canons.
Even in Hexham, Eilaf's position was by no means secure, and
in a few years time he found himself forced to retreat again
before the tide of reform. In 1113 Hexham was given to the
Austin canons, and Eilaf preserved only a life interest. Finally,
in 1138 he entered the new cathedral monastery of St Cuthbert in the presence of his three sons.[3]

Aelred, one of those three sons, was born about 1110, not
long after the time Eilaf was forced to move from Durham
to Hexham. His monastic vocation, and that of his brother
and sister, can thus be seen as a sort of completion of the
tendencies which disturbed their father's career. It would not

2. Christopher Brooke, "Gregorian Reform in Action: Clerical Marriage in
England 1050-1200" in *Medieval Church and Society* (New York, 1972), pp.
69-99.

3. R. L. Graeme Ritchie, *The Normans in Scotland* (Edinburgh, 1954), pp.
246-255, and Squire, *Aelred*, pp. 10-11.

be fair, however, to suggest that even in 1100 the career of a respectably married priest carried much social stigma with it. Eilaf had many connections among the lay and clerical aristocracy of Northumbria, and it was to these he turned when the question of 'Aelred's upbringing came to the fore about 1125.

There had been a tradition of learning in Aelred's family as far back as we can trace their story, at least since the days of Alfred, Aelred's great-grandfather, who had been a teacher at the boys school in Durham. We have no details of Aelred's earliest training, but it is more than likely that he learned the rudiments of Latin letters from a priest of Hexham, and may even have had the benefit of lessons from his uncle Aldred who later had a reputation for learning at Durham.[4]

It was the custom of the first feudal age that sons of good family should receive at least a part of their training in the homes of other members of the upper class.[5] This custom of fosterage was designed both to train the young in the manners appropriate to their station and also to provide the links of acquaintance and friendship which were so vital to the exercise of power and responsibility. Aelred was sent, at some date probably about his fifteenth year, to no mean foster home, the court of the King of Scots.

Political events of the previous generation had introduced a Norman element into the court of Scotland, and although ruling a still very barbarous land, the Scottish court was the center of a small but active group intent on bringing the customs and advantages of Norman civilization to the North. Under King David I (1124-1153), Aelred was raised in the company of Henry,[6] the heir to the throne, and David's two stepsons Simon and Waldef, who were to become his close friends and models. (It may have been at Roxborough, where

4. Squire, *Aelred*, pp. 6-10.

5. M. Bloch, *Feudal Society* (Chicago, 1961), pp. 224-227. See also P. Ariès, *Centuries of Childhood* (New York, 1962), pp. 365-369.

6. Aelred, *Geneologia regum Anglorum* in PL 195:736D: "*Cum quo ab ipsis cunabulis vixi, et puer cum puero crevi, cuius etiam adolescentiam adolescens agnovi.*"

the ambulatory Scottish court was frequently in residence, that Aelred's somewhat rough sounding Anglo-Saxon name of Ethelred was softened to the Norman form with which we are more familiar.)

We know only two facets of Aelred's years of education with certainty: In the first place, either at Hexham or at Roxborough Aelred became familiar with Cicero's dialogue *On Friendship* which was to mean so much to him in the course of his later life.[7] Secondly, he quickly became a popular and respected member of the court circle. Walter Daniel, Aelred's biographer, tells us that Aelred was appointed "dapifer summus" of the royal court,[8] and a great deal of ingenuity has been expended trying to discover the precise implications of this title.[9] It seems clear that Walter Daniel is trying to give the impression that Aelred was High Steward of Scotland, but even if the words will bear that interpretation, it seems unlikely that so young a boy would have been appointed to an office which was already becoming a major feudal responsibility. Aelred himself inclined to joke about his responsibilities as steward, insisting that his youth trained him more for work among the pots and pans in the kitchen than for writing,[10] but it is hardly necessary to see Aelred in the role of a cookboy. On the whole some position such as steward of the royal table, perhaps in charge of the general arrangements for feasts and entertainments, seems the most likely position for him to have filled.

Whatever the exact nature of his position, there can be no doubt that Aelred's life at court was a success from any worldly point of view. There he had opportunities to develop those emotional and profound friendships, for which he had such genius, with the most important and most civilized people in the kingdom. Aelred became the intimate friend of at

7. Aelred, *Spiritual Friendship*, Prologue: 2

8. *Walter Daniel's Life of Ailred* ed. F. M. Powicke, Nelson's Medieval Texts (London, 1950), pp. 3-4. Cited as *Life.*

9. *Ibid.* pp. xl-xli, and Squire, *Aelred* p. 14.

10. Aelred, *Mirror of Charity* Introduction: 2. Bernard wrote, evidently refering to an excuse given by Aelred: *Causas tuae impossibilitatis ostendisti, dicenste minus gramaticum, imo pene illiteratum, qui de coquinis, non de scholis of heremam veneris. . . .*

least one member of the court,[11] and soon found that his courtly success was to be rewarded with a great ecclesiastical benefice, perhaps the archbishopric of St Andrews.[12]

But for all this success, Aelred was not entirely happy in the life of the court. He was oppressed by the lack of a clear sense of his vocation, and disturbed by the evident superficiality of many of his relationships. In his own words: "And those men who were around me, but who were ignorant of the things which went on within me, kept saying, 'How lucky he is, how lucky he is.' But they did not know that there was evil in me, where only good should be. Terrible was the distress I felt within myself, tormenting me, corrupting my soul with intolerable stench. And unless you had quickly stretched out your hand, not being able to tolerate myself, I might have taken the most desperate remedy of despair."[13]

This has the authentic ring of the sleepless nights of a young nobleman, confident of his powers but unable to find the right way in which to put them to use. It may also betray the over-wrought language of the court, and perhaps even a trace of that religion of love which was beginning to penetrate into the courts of France, and whose mirror image was to inform the sermons of St Bernard and the Cistercian Fathers of the first golden age.[14]

While in this mood of restlessness and inner distress, Aelred was sent on a mission to York, on some business concerning Archbishop Thurstan. In 1132, only two years before this, Thurstan had assisted at the foundation of Rievaulx, a colony

11. Aelred, *Mirror of Charity* I: 79

12. Walter Daniel, *Life* p. 3: "Whence the King loved him exceedingly and every day was considering how to advance him, so much so, indeed, that if he had not unexpectedly entered the Cistercian order he would have honoured him with the first bishopric of the land.

13. Aelred, *Mirror of Charity* I: 79: "*Et dicebant homines, attendentes quaedam circa me, sed nescientes quid ageretur in me: O quam bene est illi! O quam bene est illi! Ignorabant enim, quia ibi mihi male erat, ubi solum poterat bene esse. Valde enim intus erat plaga mea, crucians, terrens, et intolerabili fetore omnia interiora mea corrumpens; et nisi cito admouisses manum, non tolerans meipsum, forte pessimum desperationis remedium adhibuissem.*"

14. Aelred knew some of the popular Arthurian romances, since he referred to *fabulis quae vulgo de nescio quo finguntur Arthuro* in *Mirror of Charity* 2:51. On courtly love and Cistercian mysticism, see E. Gilson, *The Mystical Theology of St Bernard* (London, 1940), pp. 170-197.

of monks from Citeaux sponsored by Walter Espec, a promi-
nent border lord. A few months later Thurstan had taken a
part in the painful business of settling the schism at St Mary's,
York, which led to the foundation of the great abbey of Foun-
tains by the stricter party of the monks.[15] In both these affairs
the Archbishop had supported the monks who wished to lead
their monastic life under the strictest of observances, and
whatever the subject of Aelred's official business, it seems
likely that there was conversation about the wonderful and
exciting events which were turning the wilds of Yorkshire into
a paradise of monks.

In any case, on his return journey from York, Aelred spent
a night at Walter Espec's castle at Helmsley, and the next day
rode over to Rievaulx to see the new monastery for himself.
He was profoundly impressed, and discussed the day's events
with some of his companions when they returned to Helmsely
to spend a second night. The next morning Aelred took his
life into his hands, and offered himself at the gates of Rievaulx
to become a monk.[16]

For Aelred the next few years must have been difficult,
but in some sense a homecoming. For a delicate and courtly
young man the severe discipline and rough labor of a strug-
gling monastic community must have been a heavy burden.
For a sensitive and spiritually aware young man, filled with
enthusiasm and troubled by the superficialities of the royal
court, this would have been an initiation into that profound
peace which he had found so elusive. Aelred was as immediate
a success at the monastic life as he had been at the court.
While still a relatively young man of about thirty-two, profes-
sed for no more than six years, Aelred was sent to Rome as
the proctor of his abbot in the complicated legal controversy
over the election of William, the treasurer of York, as the successor to Archbishop Thurstan.[17]

15. David Knowles, *The Monastic Order in England* (2nd ed.; Cambridge,
England, 1963), pp. 231-239. Cited as *Monastic Order*.

16. Walter Daniel, *Life* pp. 10-16.

17. David Knowles, "The Case of St William of York" in *The Historian and
Character* (Cambridge, England, 1963), pp. 76-97.

The visit to Rome seems to have made little impression on Aelred, as he makes no mention of it in his works, but on the way his route took him to Clairvaux, where he met the "chimaera of his age," St Bernard. Once again Aelred made a strikingly favorable impression, and Bernard did not forget both the spiritual depth and the literary promise of the young monk from the distant North.

On his return from the mission to Rome, Aelred was appointed master of novices, a position of great responsibility, especially in the early days of the monastery when the whole tone of the community could be altered in a few years by the torrent of young monks who applied for admission. One of Aelred's duties as novice master was to give short conferences on the meaning of the monastic life, perhaps continuing those early literary efforts which had impressed St Bernard. At first these conferences were probably only noted on wax tablets, or outlined on spare scraps of parchment from the scriptorium. But soon there came a letter from Bernard himself, ordering Aelred to digest his notes into a book, to be called the *Mirror of Charity*.[18]

Aelred had probably only begun this work of editing when he was selected to lead the party of monks setting out in 1143 to found the new abbey of Revesby. It may seem surprising that a monk of only about thirty-three years, whose only previous position in his monastery had been the brief tenure of the mastership of novices, should be given the responsibility for the foundation of a new monastery, but in those days of enthusiasm talented and devoted young men soon found their way to the positions of highest responsibility. St Bernard himself had been only twenty-four when he was appointed first abbot of Clairvaux, and many of his contemporaries were not much older when they took up the abbatial staff.

We know almost nothing of Aelred's rule at Revesby, though we may be confident that amidst his constant labors Aelred continued to work at the sermons and notes which seem to

18. A. Wilmart, "L'instigateur du *Speculum caritatis*," *Revue d'ascétique et de mystique* XIV (1933) 371-395.

have been considered a vital part of the responsibilities of an abbot, charged with building up his monks as much as building a monastery. That both labors were successful is proven by the call he received in 1147 to return to Rievaulx as abbot, upon the resignation of Maurice, who had found the burdens of rule too heavy.

It is in the period shortly after his election as abbot of Rievaulx that we should place the beginnings of the *Spiritual Friendship*. The scene of the first book is set in some monastery dependent on Rievaulx, where Aelred had intimate friends. The most likely place in Wardon, since one of the speakers in the first book is probably to be identified with the Ivo of Wardon to whom Aelred dedicated his treatise, "Jesus at the age of Twelve."[19] Aelred's regular visitation of his daughter house would be an appropriate occasion for a discussion of spiritual friendship. But after an ambitious start, the work seems to have been put aside as the responsibilities of a busy Cistercian abbot took precedence, and it was not resumed for almost twenty years.

In the interval we must imagine Aelred as almost constantly in motion. As abbot he was responsible not only for the administration of his own monastery, which grew under his care from three hundred to over six hundred choir monks and lay-brothers,[20] but also for the paternal supervision of the many daughter houses which Rievaulx sent out to colonize Yorkshire and the Borders. A single year would have taken Aelred from Dundrennan, in the wild Celtic country of Galloway, to Melrose in the Scottish border country, and south to Wardon in Bedforshire. In addition he would have made the laborious pilgrimage overseas to the General Chapter at Citeaux, probably calling on the way at Clairvaux, Rievaulx' mother house. It was only in his last years, his health much undermined both by the rigors of the climate and his own penances, that Aelred received permission to mitigate some of his duties, and possibly to delegate his visitations.[21]

19. Aelred, "Jesus at the Age of Twelve," Cistercian Fathers Series 2 (Spencer, Mass., 1971)

20. Walter Daniel, *Life* p. 38. These figures, like most medieval estimates, may be exaggerated.

21. *Ibid.* p. 20.

As late as the fifteenth century a volume of some three hundred of Aelred's letters, written to kings, bishops and nobles, existed in England.[22] These letters might have provided information about the external events of Aelred's twenty years as abbot of Rievaulx, which Walter Daniel's *Life* does not. Walter was concerned with the life of a man whom he was certain was a saint; he recounted the miracles and prodigies of Aelred's abbacy, but gave us very little of the context of daily life which would make Aelred's sainthood seem more real to us who have lost the taste for the marvellous.

Aside from the round of visitations which we can assume Aelred kept up, not only because Walter Daniel mentions incidents which seem to have taken place during his regular travels, but because the General Chapter would have been interested if Aelred were not able to supervise the regularity of discipline, Aelred had a few known activities outside his monastery. We know that at some time he preached at a synod in Troyes; and the texts of two sermons "in synodo" survive, though without aates.[23] These sermons were probably given en route to or from the General Chapter, since Troyes is very near Clairvaux, and on the route to Citeaux.

Toward the very end of his life, Aelred was also involved in the celebrations surrounding the translation of the relics of St Edward the Confessor, whose canonization Henry II had secured with an eye to encouraging English patriotism and the reconciliation of the French and English people of his kingdom. Many authors maintain that Aelred actually came to Westminster to preach on the occasion, but in view of his poor health it seems more likely that he was not personally present. Abbot Laurence of Westminster was a distant relative of Aelred's, and asked him to compose both the homily for the new office of the saint, and to write, or at least revise, a standard life of Edward.[24] The liturgical homily which Aelred wrote does not survive, but the version of the *Life of the Confessor* which he re-worked from an older work by Osbert of Clare, adding some new material at the end, was very popular

22. *Ibid.* p. 42, and cf. p. *c.*

23. Aelred, *Sermones inediti*, ed. C. H. Talbot, Series Scriptorum S. Ordinis Cisterciensis (Rome, 1952), pp. 150-161.

24. Walter Daniel, *Life* p. 41; Squire, *Aelred* pp. 94-96.

in the middle ages, and survives in a number of manuscripts.[25]

The last work of Aelred's life seems to have been his study *De anima.*[26] According to Master Walter the work was unfinished at Aelred's death, but since the work seems to come to a logical conclusion it is possible that all that Aelred had left to do was some polishing of the style.[27] The work itself is respectable, but shows few of the remarkable qualities of perception and observation which make the *Mirror of Charity* and the *Spiritual Friendship* classics. As long as Aelred could rely on his own experience and the profound but limited literary culture of the early twelfth century, he was on firm ground and produced works of major value. But when he attempted to enter the more technical realism of philosophy, his lack of formal training in the schools, and the relative backwardness of the north of England put him at a great disadvantage. His work is an interesting re-consideration of the ideas of St Augustine, but it adds little of novelty, and in some cases even confuses the issues. In contrast, Aelred's discussion of spiritual friendship is both clear on all points and original, discussing with great perception issues which had not been treated by his masters, Augustine and the other Fathers of the monastic tradition.

For at least the last ten years of his administration, Aelred was in poor health. Walter Daniel often seems all too glad to give the details of Aelred's illnesses, which led professor Powick to suggest that Walter may have had a professional concern with Aelred's health as the infirmarian of Rievaulx.[28] Walter noted that as early as 1157, the General Chapter had allowed Aelred a number of privileges because of the infirmities which troubled him. He was allowed to live and eat in the infirmary, where he built himself a little cell which was to be the scene of many conversations with his monks, and to attend choir at his convenience. Walter vividly describes Aelred

25. Anselm Hoste, *Bibliotheca Aelrediana* (Steenbrugge, Belgium, 1962), p. 102.
26. Ed. C. H. Talbot, *Medieval and Renaissance Studies, Sup.* 1 (London, 1952).
27. *Ibid.* pp. 56-57. Cf. Walter Daniel, *Life* p. 42.
28. Walter Daniel, *Life* p. xxvii.

in the throes of an attack, probably of kidney stones, sitting by the fire, crumpled in pain like a leaf of parchment.[29]

Aelred died on 12 January 1167. His final hours were as faithful to the love of God and his friends as had been his life and teachings. Walter records his last words: "Festinate [Hasten], for crist luve." He spoke the Lord's name in English, since he found it "easier to utter, and in some ways sweeter to hear" in the language of his birth.[30]

Aelred died, as he had lived, surrounded by a crowd of his monks. For many years it had been his custom to allow his monks to come to his cell in the infirmary for familiar conversations:

> For every day they came to it and sat in it,
> twenty or thirty at a time, to talk together
> of the spiritual delights of the Scriptures
> and of the observance of the Order. There
> was nobody to say to them, "Get out, go away,
> do not touch the Abbot's bed"; they walked and
> lay about his bed and talked with him as a
> little child prattles with its mother. He
> would say to them, "My sons, say what you will;
> only let no vile word, no detration of a brother,
> no blasphemy against God proceed out of your
> mouth." He did not treat them with the
> pedantic imbecility habitual in some silly
> abbots who, if a monk takes a brother's
> hand in his own, or says anything that they
> do not like, demand his cowl, strip and expel
> him. Not so Aelred, not so.[31]

Since his days in the court of Scotland, Aelred's gentleness and compassion had caused some to resent him, thinking him soft or a hypocrite. Even after his death objections were raised to some of the incidents reported as miracles by Walter Daniel, who hastened to write a rebuttal, citing the sources of his

29. *Ibid.* p. 79: "His body, looking by the fire like a leaf of parchment, was so bent that his head seemed altogether lost between his knees."
30. *Ibid.* p. 60.
31. *Ibid.* p. 40.

stories.[32] But the overwhelming impression left behind by
Aelred was of sanctity and sanity. Continuing the tradition of
Bernard and Aelred himself,[33] Gilbert, abbot of Swineshead in
Lincolnshire, broke off his sermon in chapter to make a
moving eulogy when the news of Aelred's death was brought:

> What a honeycomb, how mighty and how rich
> a one, has passed in these days to the heavenly
> banquet. . . . It seems to me that in him, in his
> being taken from us, our garden has been stripped,
> and has given up a great sheaf of myrrh to God
> the husbandman. There is no such honeycomb
> left in our homes. His discourse was like
> the honeycomb, pouring out the honey of
> knowledge. His body was languishing with
> illness, but he himself languished more in
> spirit from love of heavenly things.[34]

Since the papacy had not yet centralized the process of
canonization at the time of his death, there was no formal
ratification by the Roman See of Aelred's sanctity. But he
has been accounted a saint by the Cistercian order, and Dom
David Knowles tell us that he was called the "Bernard of the
North."[35] If he lacked the burning singlemindedness of Bernard, he had a warmth of love which did not scorch as Bernard's sometimes did. Bernard preached a crusade and destroy-
ed Abelard for the sake of the love of God; Aelred prefered
to reconcile enemies and write of the virtue of friendship. He
was a man whose love was great enough to prove that greatness does not need to be brutal, and that to be a saint one
does not have to despise human affections. In the words of
Dom Knowles: "No other English monk of the twelfth century
so lingers in the memory; like Anselm of Bec he escapes from
his age, though most typical of it, and speaks directly to us
. . . of his restless search for One to whom he might give the
full strength of his love."[36]

32. *Ibid.* p. 66-67.
33. St Bernard had devoted most of his 26th sermon on the Song of Songs to
the death of his brother Gerard, and Aelred interrupted his *Mirror of Charity* at
1:98 to lament the death of a friend.
34. PL 184:216. The translation is from Louis Bouyer, *The Cistercian Heritage*
(Westminster, Md., 1958), pp. 130-131, slightly abridged.
35. Knowles, *Monastic Order* p. 240.
36. *Ibid.*

THE DOCTRINE OF THE *SPIRITUAL FRIENDSHIP*

THERE ARE A NUMBER OF AMBIGUITIES which make it difficult to place Aelred's *Spiritual Friendship* in the context of medieval, and especially medieval monastic, works on the subject. Mother A. M. Fisk has shown that there is indeed a considerable body of patristic and medieval spiritual writing in which friendship is discussed as a Christian virtue, a form of charity, or a symbol of the divine life of the Trinity.[1] In spite of Mother Fisk's industry, however, it is equally clear that this positive valuation of human friendship was relatively unusual, and that the tradition of the Fathers and of the monastic authors of the early middle ages was very reserved in its appreciation of the value of friendship.

In the patristic period, for example, we may be impressed by the human feeling of Paulinus of Nola's verses to his friend Ausonius,[2] and remember some of Augustine's splendid rhetoric celebrating the friendships of his youth.[3] Still, Augustine's more considered opinion seems to have been that which he declared when remembering the death of a friend: since all things mortal perish, we are better off not becoming too attached to anything or anyone except God.[4]

1. Adele M. Fisk, *Friends and Friendship in the Monastic Tradition,* Cidoc Cuaderno 51 (Cuernavaca, Mexico, 1970). Cited as *Friends.*

2. *The Oxford Book of Medieval Verse,* ed. F. J. E. Raby (Oxford, 1959), p. 31. See also P. Febre, *St Paulin de Nole et l'amitié chrétienne* (Paris, 1949), esp. pp. 137-154.

3. Augustine, *Confessions,* 6:6-10.

4. *Ibid.* 4:9.

15

Dom Jean Leclercq has made us aware that there was a very popular genre of medieval letters devoted to the expression of feelings of friendship.[5] These letters were part of the repertory of every well-trained writer, and indeed many of our surviving examples have the appearance of being schoolroom productions not intended for any particular correspondent. There is, however, a considerable body of actual correspondence, some of the most moving of which was written by St Anselm, whose purpose is the expression of friendship and the development of a theology linking human relationships with the love of God.[6]

This current of specifically monastic friendship met a great obstacle in another aspect of the monastic tradition: the firm oposition of the *Rule* of St Benedict to any "factions" which might disturb the complete unity and equality of the monastic family. The very earliest Fathers of the Desert had alternately treasured their friends as guides and helpers on the path to virtue, and rejected any personal entanglements which could keep them from the purity of heart which they prized above all. As the cenobitic tradition developed after Pachomius, monastic legislators became more suspicious of the divisive effects of "particular friendships" which could lead to favoritism and grumbling in the community. Benedict's *Rule* says nothing about friendship explicitly, but insists on taciturnity, the absolute equality of all monks in a hierarchy of respect based entirely upon office and date of profession, and resolutely condemns "murmuring" or the formation of factions.[7] All this hardly encourages the sort of intense personal relationships which Augustine and Anselm occasionally celebrated.

It is also difficult to doubt that fear of homosexuality dis-

5. Jean Leclercq, "L'amitié dans les lettres au moyen âge," *Revue du moyen âge latin*, I (1945), 391-410, and the same author's *The Love of Learning and the Desire for God* (New York, 1961), pp. 226-227.

6. R. W. Southern, *St Anselm and his Biographer* (Cambridge, England, 1963), pp. 67-76.

7. *Regula monachorum sancti Benedicti,* ed. Ph. Schmitz, (Maredsous, Belgium, 1955). See especially c. 6 (taciturnity), c. 63 (order of precedence), and c. 69 (the danger of factions). Cited as *RB.*

couraged monastic acceptance of the particular friendship. There is very little explicit discussion of the subject in the monastic litterature,[8] but both the penitentials of the early middle ages and the moral literature of the high middle ages indicate that homosexuality was considered a serious and dangerous vice. Consciously aware of it or not, no religious superior could have been unconcerned to find an intimate personal relationship developing between two of his subjects.

These, then, are some of the questions which must be considered before we can understand Aelred's *Spiritual Friendship*. How did Aelred see the relationship between friendship with mortal men and with the immortal God? How did he reconcile his favorable evaluation of particular friendships for monks with the danger of factionalism within the monastic community? And how did he deal with the possibility that an emotional relationship in a closed community might provide an occasion for sexual temptation?

A superficial reading of the *Spiritual Friendship* could give the impression that Aelred was either so optimistic about human nature as to have overlooked these problems entirely, or so pessimistic as to have made friendship safe by making it a matter of pure abstraction and calculation. But the very diversity of these impressions should give the warning that Aelred's doctrine of spiritual friendship is rich and complex enough to deal with the complexity of real relationships in an authentic manner. It is certainly true that Aelred is enthusiastic about friendship: he insists on the usefulness of friendship as part of the good life, and stated flatly: "I call them more beasts than men, who say life should be led so that they need not console anyone nor occasion distress or sorrow to anyone, who take no pleasure in the good of an other nor expect their failures to distress others, seeking to love no one and be loved by none."[9] He even proposed the rather shocking formula, "God is friendship" and justified it on the grounds

8. D. Chitty, *The Desert a City* (Oxford, 1966), pp. 66-67 gives references to the teachings of the monastic fathers of Egypt on the subject.
9. Aelred, Spir amic 2:9-14 and 2:52

that "He who dwells in friendship dwells in God, and God in him."[10] On the other hand, it is also clear that Aelred was no misty-eyed romantic about personal relations. He knew that there were many imperfect or even totally corrupt relationships which went under the guise of friendship, and insisted that before becoming committed to a friend a great deal of consideration and testing was essential if vice and disaster were to be avoided.

Moreover, Aelred's discussion of friendship can only be understood as a special case of his more general theory of love, which he had developed in his first work, the *Mirror of Charity*. Before attempting any detailed analysis of the teaching on friendship, it would be a good idea to take a quick glance at Aelred's general theory of love and will.[11]

It should be no surprise that Aelred began his careful analysis of love by dividing it into three parts: attraction, intention and fruition.[12] The attraction is that natural impression made in our mind by some person or object, which we can identify as being desirable. The intention is more abstract: it is the inclination of the will towards some person or object as the result of the decision that it ought to be followed. The fruition is the result of this act of the will by which we enjoy the benefits of that object of our sensible attraction and volitional decision.

Aelred knew that if it were not for original sin, i.e. if man were still uncorrupted, no further analysis would be necessary. But since man is corrupt, it is possible for each of these three parts of love to be defective: man can be attracted to the wrong object, can decide to pursue that which he knows is wrong, and can enjoy created goods incorrectly. If any of these corruptions vitiate the goodness of his love it ceases to be love and becomes cupidity instead.

10. *Ibid.* 1:69-70. The allusions are to I Jn 4:16.
11. See Amédée Hallier, *The Theology of Aelred of Rievaulx: an Experiential Theology*. Cistercian Studies 2 (Spencer, Mass., 1969) pp. 26-33.
12. Aelred, Spec car 3:22. See *De speculo caritatis*, ed. A. Hoste, Corpus christianorum, continuatio mediaevalis, 1 (Turnhout, Belgium, 1971), pp. 115: *Constat autem, ut mihi videtur, usus eius |amoris| in tribus; in electione, in motu, in fructu. Est autem electio ex ratione, motus in desiderio et actu, fructus in fine.*

In this scheme there is no danger of a Manichean rejection of the material world, or even of a devaluation of creation in favor of the Creator. Love is still pure if it is directed toward a neighbor and not to God directly, as long as it is properly enjoyed. And though the only measure of our love for God is to love him without measure, the essential nature of our attraction, and fruition of God does not fundamentally differ from our love of neighbor. Indeed, if our love of God is corrupted by loving him for the wrong reason, such as for the benefits he can give us, it too can become a kind of cupidity.

Beyond the ever present danger that we may corrupt our love into cupidity by seeking the wrong objects to love, or loving them out of proportion to their true value, there is the difficulty which our corrupt natures have in feeling satisfaction at loving the good. We know that we ought to love our enemies and can sometimes even understand why they are worthy of our love, but our sinful natures will not allow us to feel the attraction which we know with our minds. In cases like this, we must rely on our wills, deciding to love where we feel no attraction, just as in other cases we must decide to reject an attraction which our senses present, since we know it to be unreasonable. It is only in heaven, when our senses have been purified and our wills made straight that we will be able to love with perfect freedom.[13]

In this world, however, there is a special form of love which comes closer to the love of the saints in heaven than most others: the love of friendship. We have a clear duty to love all men, and especially our immediate neighbors. For the monk, this means especially the members of his community. But it is also clear that no one, not even the best monk, can find all the members of his community enjoyable; there will be some whom he must love as an act of the will and intellect, without the consolation of being able to enjoy his company. Towards others, however, all things will work together to produce a kind of love which is a foretaste of heaven: the attrac-

13. Aelred, Spec car 3:107-108.

tion, intention, and enjoyment will satisfy not only his judgement of what is right, but also his feelings of what is enjoyable.

By carefully distinguishing between love and cupidity Aelred was thus able to make a clear distinction between true friendship, which can only come from true love, and false friendships which are based on some imperfect or even corrupt love, and which are referred to as friendships only by the abuse of popular speech. By insisting on the positive moral value of friendship, Aelred avoided the problem of defining its moral limits, a problem which had troubled Cicero and other ancient writers who thought of friendship as purely amoral. Since true friendship can only be based on true love, there can be no admixture of corrupt motives. There can be no question of unjust favoritism, much less partnership in vice, for true friends, since motives of gain or corrupt pleasure are characteristic of false friendship and have no place in a relationship of true, spiritual friendship.

On the other hand, Aelred is far too acute an observer of human nature to suggest that a spiritual friendship between two mortals does not need to be carefully tended to weed out those seeds of corruption which are natural to our fallen state.[14] It is essential, therefore, that the spiritual man both carefully test himself and the person whose friendship he desires to be sure that the natural materials for a friendship are pure, and be prepared to renounce the personal satisfactions of friendship (though never the good will which we owe all men) if a spiritual friendship is corrupted into a carnal or self-seeking relationship.[15]

With these preconditions in mind, we can begin to answer some of the questions posed earlier about Aelred's understanding of monastic friendship. For Aelred there can be no conflict between love of our friends and the love of God, since all love is one and has its source in God. The love of neighbor is no derogation of our love of God, but rather is necessary for us

14. As Gerson expressed the idea: *Spiritualis amor facile labitur in nudum carnalem amorem.* See J. Huizinga, *The Waning of the Middle Ages* (London, 1924) p. 178.
15. Aelred, Spec car 3:43-47; Spir amic 3:39-44.

if we are truly to love him. It is this identification of spiritual friendship with the perfect love of God which allowed Aelred to suggest the phrase, "God is friendship." In the same way, since the monastery is a school of love, there can be no possibility in the monastery of love causing factions. Cupidity can indeed be devisive and false friendships, based on cupidity instead of charity, are even more dangerous for a monk than for people in the world, but true love builds up the community and can only serve to unify, not tear apart.

The final question, of Aelred's attitude toward the sexual component of intimate personal relationships, is far more difficult to answer. Aelred was, of course, not troubled by the twentieth century's pervasive consiousness of sexual drives, nor did he feel obliged to discuss sexual pathology in a treatise on spiritual friendship. It is possible, however, to get a glimpse of his implicit attitude from remarks in the *Spiritual Friendship,* and from Walter Daniel's biography.

The description which Aelred himself gave of his inner distress during his last period at the Scottish court is extremely vague,[16] but it is at least possible to interpret his relationship of great intimacy and youthful passion in the light of the remarks about "carnal" friendships in the *Spiritual Friendship.* There may well have been a homosexual component to his youthful friendship which he found very disturbing, even if he was not fully aware of its implications.[17] In this case, his conversion to the monastic life might have been, to at least some degree, a method of escaping a potentially sexual situation of which he could not morally approve. The later evidence of Aelred's life would seem to indicate, however, that if this was the case, Aelred suffered no emotional damage from the experience. The close and very emotional friendships which he was able to enjoy in the monastery prove that a negative reaction to his own youthful crush on a member of the court of Scotland did not inhibit his emotional freedom in later life. It is also interesting to remember that Walter Daniel specifically noted that Aelred, unlike some other abbots, was not

16. Aelred. Spec car 1:79-82.
17. Aelred, Spir amic 1:38-41 and 2:57-58.

scandalized by demonstrations of affection, such as holding hands, by his monks. Aelred, in other words, seems to have had not only confidence in his own ability to deal with the sexual component of his friendships, but to have trusted his monks to be able to do the same. Nor is there any evidence that Aelred's confidence was misplaced.

With these preliminary considerations in mind, it is possible to look at the structure of the work itself. The introduction of the second book makes clear that the *Spiritual Friendship* was begun early, probably sometime in the early 1140's.[18] Then in 1164, a date which can be established by a reference to the disputed election of Pope Paschal III, the work was resumed and completed before Aelred's death in 1167.[19] As might be expected, there is a certain amount of repetition, and even a few points on which Aelred seems to have changed his mind in the course of the twenty years between the first notes and the completion of the work, but on the whole the work shows a remarkable unity and sense of form.

The plan of the work is very simple, and follows in broad outline that of Cicero's *De amicitia,* upon which it is explicitly modeled.[20] The first book treats of the origin and essence of friendship, the second goes on to consider the utility and limits of friendship, and the third concludes with some rather random remarks about practical difficulties. The form of the work is the Ciceronian dialogue, with the characters very carefully realized, but with Aelred himself almost always providing the answers to questions posed by the other interlocutors.

At the beginning of the first book, after a short prologue introducing himself and telling of his youthful interest in Cicero's books, Aelred proposed beginning the consideration of friendship by taking Cicero's definition as a provisional working model. Cicero had described friendship as: Agreement on matters human and divine, with charity and good will.[21]

18. Aelred, Spir amic 2:5. Cf. *L'amitié spirituelle,* ed. and trans. J. Dubois (Paris-Bruges, 1948) pp. xcii-cv.

19. Aelred, Spir amic 2:41 refers to the schism of Octavian.

20. *Ibid.* Prologue.

21. *Ibid.* 1:11. See Cicero, *De amicitia* 6:20: *Est enim amicitia nihil aliud nisi omnium divinarum humanarumque rerum cum benevolentia et caritate consensio.*

By "good will" Aelred understood Cicero to mean a rational and voluntary choice to benefit someone, and by "charity" the enjoyment of our natural affection toward someone.[22] Thus Aelred read his own distinction between the rational and irrational parts of properly ordered love into the words which Cicero probably meant as synonyms.

Aelred looked at friendship from the divine perspective, insisting that it springs directly from God, who in the overflowing of his love created men to share his love by loving each other and himself. This opportunity for love, which extends to a certain extent even to irrational creatures, is the particular glory of men and angels. Man's nature thus requires that he be a loving as well as a rational creature. Aelred says: "Nature impresses on the human heart the inclination toward friendship. Then experience encourages it, and the authority of the law regulates it."[23]

This reference to the regulation of the law points to a very practical aspect of Aelred's work. Like his master St Augustine, Aelred was very aware of man's fall into original sin, and never failed to take sin into account. In the world as it ought to have been, there would have been no distinction between charity and friendship: we would have freely and properly loved our neighbor, and in enjoying this love the law would have had no claim on us. But now that man is fallen, we must always be on our guard against false loves, which are cupidity not charity, and false friendships, which are a species of cupidity. There is no single name which distinguishes these false friendships from the only true kind, which Aelred called "spiritual friendship," but Aelred gave several lists of these pseudo-friendships in which disordered and excessive affections offend against the law.

The two broad headings under which these false friendships fall are the friendship for carnal pleasure and the friendship for material gain. Each of these offends by rejecting one of the components of true friendship, according to the defini-

22. Aelred, Spir amic 1:19-21.
23. *Ibid*. 1:51.

tion taken from Cicero. Carnal friendship offends against "good will," since when we indulge in sin we hate our own souls and those we involve in sin. Self-seeking friendship, on the other hand, offends against "charity," since it simulates an affection toward a person which is really felt only toward his goods.[24]

The only true friendship is that which combines the two vital elements of charity and good will in the consensus on things human and divine. True friendship is the perfection of false friendships, not their opposite. Carnal friendship has a sort of charity in its enjoyment of a natural affection, but lacks good will; self-seeking friendship has the rational choice necessary for good will but lacks the charity. It is only spiritual friendship which combines both charity and good will, a perfect consensus of things human and divine.

Since God built a need for love into our nature, even evil men feel a need for false friendship as a solace in their misery. The existance of these associations of evil, wrongly called friendships, has tended to obscure the fact that friendship is a virtue and indeed the practical expression of love as it ought to be between all men. As a result of original sin, men can reach the perfection of friendship with only a few, but this unhappy situation will be changed when all the effects of sin are removed after the last Judgement. Then we will see that the life of the just will be the life of spiritual friendship. It is in this context that Aelred paraphrased St John, and suggested that, "He who abides in friendship abides in God, and God in him."[25]

Aelred was not prepared to take up the problem which had troubled all the ancient moralists: what are the moral limits of "good will" in friendship? Aelred began with the saying of Jesus, "Greater love has no man than this, that he lay down his life for his friends."[26] Aelred understood this to mean that there is no limit to true friendship, as long as it remains true by observing the law. Since friendship is love, immoral actions are a kind of hatred, not friendship at all. With Cicero, Aelred

24. *Ibid.* 1:34-43.
25. *Ibid.* 1:70.
26. Jn 15:13.

insisted that friendship is possible only between good men, who reject sin and greed which would turn friendship into hate.[27] It is thus impossible to prefer a friend to morality; as soon as morality is damaged, friendship vanishes.

Having thus defined the nature, origins, and limits of friendship, Aelred proceeded to discuss its delights and the means of its cultivation. Gratian, one of the interlocutors in the second and third books, suggested that since men are inclined to evil, true friendship may be impossible, or at least possible for only a heroic few. Aelred replied with vigor to this suggestion.[28] No superhuman degree of goodness is necessary for true friendship. Even though the affections are difficult to control, this virtue, like all Christian virtues, is available to anyone who humbly seeks it. To renounce friendship as too difficult is not only to renounce virtue, but even true humanity, since "to live without friendship is to live like a beast."[29]

Aelred also took the occasion to repeat and develop his idea of true friendship in contrast to the false friendships which he had defined in the first book. After repeating the rejection of carnal, here called "childish," friendship in almost the same words as he had used many years before, Aelred discussed the sort of simple comradeship which Gratian proposed as being much easier and less demanding of heroic virtue than true spiritual friendship. This simple comaraderie is a sort of childish friendship, Aelred insisted, but as long as there is no admixture of vice it should be tolerated in the hope that it will grow into a genuine spiritual friendship. It may be possible to see a certain growth of Aelred's tolerance in this qualified acceptance of a sort of false friendship which in his more strenuous youth he had rejected out of hand.[30]

The final book of the *Spiritual Friendship* is concerned primarily with the practical business of making and keeping friends. Aelred was regretfully aware that even in a monastery not everyone was capable of a spiritual friendship with every-

27. Aelred, Spir amic 2:38-41.
28. *Ibid.* 2:43-44.
29. *Ibid.* 2:52.
30. *Ibid.* 3:85-87.

one else, and that certain people can be made friends only with great difficulty.

The sort of person whom Aelred found most unapt for true friendship is one easily given to anger—the choleric man of medieval medical theory.[31] Since the goal of friendship is that peace and relaxation which is the result of the calm enjoyment of love, the choleric man, given to sudden suspicious and unreasonable fits of anger, is the most difficult to relax with and enjoy. However, even granting this, Aelred was unwilling to deprive even the most unlikely sorts of all possibility of friendship. One of the dialogue's speakers pointed out that Aelred himself had a friend well-known for his choleric temper, a point which Aelred admitted with complaisance.[32] With that buoyant optimism which seemed to come so easily to the early Cistercians, Aelred insisted that faults of character, even those which come from our natural temper, are not beyond the action of grace and freewill. It is true that his friend is bad tempered, and even gives offense to Aelred himself. But there is nevertheless a fund of good will in him, and as long as that good will is not affected, all the advantages of friendship are still available to him.

In spite of this optimism, however, Aelred did admit that there were certain circumstances which required the breaking off of a friendship, at least as far as active intimacy was concerned. Aelred took a passage from Sirach and interpreted it to suggest that there were five things which would break the bonds of friendship: insult, attack, arrogance, betrayal of secrets, and the stab in the back.[33] To these Aelred added one more of his own, typical of his concern for the community entrusted to him as abbot: harm done to anyone for whom we have responsibility.[34]

In admitting that there are cases in which a friendship may have to be broken off, Aelred was faced with the text which he had quoted several times from St Jerome: "A friendship

---

31. C. S. Lewis, *The Discarded Image* (Cambridge, England, 1970) pp. 169-173.
32. Aelred, Spir amic 3:17-20 and 33-38.
33. *Ibid.* 3:23-26. The reference is to Sir 22:25-27.
34. *Ibid.* 3-46.

which can cease to be was never genuine."[35] His solution to this difficulty is ingenious and subtle. He suggested that there is a sense in which friendship can never be broken, since the obligation to love, of which friendship is only a perfect form, exists even toward enemies. We have therefore, an obligation to persist in that good will which is of the essence of friendship even toward those whom we can no longer trust with intimacy. It is only the natural affection, essential to friendship here on earth, which is broken off, and even that will (one hopes) be restored in heaven when all our love is made perfect.[36]

The necessity of breaking off an intimacy is a painful and unpleasant business, and Aelred judged that it could usually be avoided by careful testing of acquaintances before admitting them to intimacy. This process of testing and training sounds very like a novitiate, for the good reason that both have a very similar purpose. The monastery is the school of charity, in which the monk learns "to run with the unspeakable sweetness of love in the way of God's commandments."[37] The Cistercian Order too, founded on the Charter of Charity, is a society of independent monasteries bound in a filial and friendly relationship. It is only reasonable therefore that just as the monk must be tested and learn the rule of love in the monastery, and as each monastery must be visited and tested to see that the relationship of the Order does not break down, so there must be testing and correction in the formation of a friendship.

Many people, including some monks, found the exacting standards which the Cistercians required of monks to be too rigorous for mortal flesh. In the same way Walter, one of the speakers in the dialogue, proposed that a less exacting standard be allowed, requiring less testing and allowing a wider circle of comradeship. In the best Cistercian spirit, Aelred rejected this suggestion as unworthy of the true sublimity of

---

35. *Ibid.* 3:48. The quotation is Jerome, Letter 3:6: *Amicitia quae desinere potest numquam vera fuit.* (PL 22:335A).
36. Aelred, Spir amic 3:51-52.
37. RB Prologue.

friendship.[38] In friendship, as in the monastic life, the Cistercians were not satisfied with the second class. Aelred insisted that although the effort might seem a little harsh at first, the rewards of perfect spiritual friendship were more than worth a little strenuous effort at the start.[39]

Having thus cleared up the last major obstacle to the practice of true friendship, Aelred proceeded to tie up a few loose ends. A few pages suffice to remind his audience that a perfect equality is necessary between friends, and to reply to the objection that the monk, who has no property is prevented from giving gifts of friendship. For Aelred, this is an advantage, not an obstacle, since it removes all temptation to profit from a friendship, but allows the monk to offer those spiritual gifts of prayer and good example which are the most precious of all.[40]

The conclusion of this last book is a personal meditation on the memory of two of Aelred's dearest friends who preceded him to the grave. The obvious warmth of these relationships allowed Aelred to demonstrate that in spite of the rather cool prudence which has dominated the counsels just given, his own affections were not purely intellectual. These reminiscences are the final witness that Aelred's reasoning was based on his own passionate experience, proceeding from the heart as well as the head.

38. Aelred, Spir amic 3:85-87.

39. RB Prologue: *Constituenda est ergo nobis Dominici scola servitii: in qua institutione nihil asperum, nihil grave nos constituros speramus. Sed et si quid paululum restrictius, dictante aequitatis ratione, propter emendationem vitiorum vel conservationem caritatis processerit, non ilico pavore perterritus, refugias viam salutis, quae non est nisi angusto initio incipienda.*

40. Aelred, Spir amic 3:101-102.

SOURCES OF THE *SPIRITUAL FRIENDSHIP*

IT IS NOT NECESSARY to make an elaborate investigation to discover Aelred's basic source for the *Spiritual Friendship*; at the very beginning of the book he recounts his discovery of Cicero's *De amicitia* while still a schoolboy and the profound impression which the work made on him.[1] Considering that the work was very popular in the eleventh and twelfth centuries, it is not surprising that Aelred should have seen it. (We still possess the copy from the Durham library which Aelred may have read.)[2] But it is a bit surprising that a work so essentially secular in character should have continued to make such an impression on Aelred after his conversion, when, as he notes himself, nothing which was not "salted with the Scriptures" was to his taste.[3] But for Aelred, Cicero's *De amicitia* had served a function very like that which the *Hortensius* served for Augustine, turning him from trifles toward God, and Aelred never put Cicero by, as Augustine had the *Hortensius,* in his rather more drawn-out progress toward sainthood.

A glance at the notes, especially of the second and third books of the *Spiritual Friendship,* will show how thoroughly Aelred relied on Cicero. There is hardly a page on which some quotation or at least some allusion to the *De amicitia* does not appear. It is estimated that fully one third of Cicero's work is

1. Aelred, Spir amic Prologue: 2.
2. Squire, *Aelred,* p. 101.
3. Aelred, Spir amic Prologue: 5.

29

contained in Aelred's.[4] Cicero's influence, however, goes even beyond the substance of the arguments, since the very form of Aelred's work is in great part derived from the *De amicitia.* Cicero divided his subject into three parts, the nature, advantages and laws of friendship, and Aelred observed a similar arrangement of the discussion in his three books. Likewise, although there are only two speakers in the first, and least Ciceronian, book of the *Spiritual Friendship,* the last two books have the same number of speakers as Cicero and leave the greater part of the discussion to the central authority figure. The works even close in the same fashion, with Cicero giving an account of his protagonist's friendship with Scipio, and Aelred speaking of his own monastic friendships. However, though Aelred took Cicero for his master in the matter and even in the outline of the *Spiritual Friendship,* he did not hesitate to adapt him when he was insufficiently Christian, and even to differ with him on some points. Thus in the definition of friendship which is quoted directly from Cicero, Aelred made it clear that he used it only provisionally, and felt free to drop the qualification "all" from Cicero's phrase "agreement on all matters human and divine."[5] On an even more basic point, Aelred differed with Cicero when the *De amicitia* fell short of Christian standards: Cicero had suggested that we should follow the wishes of a friend, "even if by some chance the wishes of a friend are not altogether honorable, . . . provided, however, that utter disgrace does not follow."[6] Aelred rejected this opinion with vigor in the name of his more developed understanding of friendship as a species of true charity: "Therefore their opinion is to be detested who think that one may work for a friend against faith or honor."[7]

Behind this general consensus with Cicero lies hidden Aelred's general agreement with the whole tradition of Greek ethical philosophy. Cicero's own sources are mysterious, though a lost work by Theophrastus has been suggested. A general resemblance in outline to Aristotle's *Nicheomachean Ethics* is

---

4. Dubois, *L'amitié spirituelle,* p. li.
5. Cicero, Amic 6:10. Ed. and trans. William Falconer, Loeb Classical Library, (Cambridge, Mass., 1959), p. 130.
6. Cicero, Amic 17:61. *Ed. cit.,* p. 170.
7. Aelred, Spir amic 2:39.

clear, though it is likely that Cicero did not know this work directly. Aelred himself could not go behind Cicero, and we need not either.[8]

The Scriptures and the writings of the Fathers are the second of the major sources of Aelred's ideas. In so far as his sources have been identified, Aelred's familiarity with the Fathers does not seem to have been extraordinarily wide, but he had made a profound study of a few major patristic authors whose works were available to him.

Among the Fathers, Augustine was clearly Aelred's favorite, and his favorite among Augustine's works was undoubtedly the *Confessions.* Walter Daniel tells us that Aelred "generally had in his hands the *Confessions* of Augustine, for it was these which had been his guide when he was converted from the world."[9] Walter also reports that at the time of Aelred's death the books which he had in his private oratory were a Psalter, the Gospel of John, and the *Confessions.* It comes as no surprise therefore that Aelred painted his own youth in Augustinian terms, describing his overwhelming desire to "love and be loved."[10] The model of human psychology which Aelred used is also Augustinian in its outline, although that dependence is clearer when he is discussing such matters explicitly in his *De anima.* As a result, his *Spiritual Friendship* gives the impression of a thoroughly Augustinian structure, built on the foundation provided by Cicero. The doctrine is expressed in scriptural and patristic terms but is no more a *florilegium* of the Fathers than it is a simple copy of Cicero.

Aelred was aware that the Fathers sometimes differed from Cicero and from each other, and he was willing to differ from certain parts of the patristic tradition. Thus, in spite of his devotion to Augustine, and the particular delight he took in the *Confessions,* Aelred felt free to express a far higher valuation of human friendship than Augustine had allowed after the death of his friend.[11]

8. Dubois, *L'amitié spirituelle* p. lii-lv.

9. Walter Daniel, *Life*, p. 50.

10. Aelred, Spir amic Prologue:1; Augustine, *Confessions* 2:2. See also P. Courcelle, "Aelred de Rievaulx à l'école des *Confessions*" *Revue des Etudes Augustiniennes* 3 (1957), 163-174.

11. See the previous section on the doctrine of Spir amic, esp. notes 3 and 4.

For all his dependence upon Cicero and St Augustine, Aelred was sufficiently in command of his sources to be able to suggest graceful syntheses of his often differing and highly sophisticated materials. He resolved the conflict between Jerome's assertion that true friendship is eternal and the careful directions Cicero gave for breaking off an intolerable relationship by insisting that although the love of friendship is eternal, vice or malice may destroy the affection which is the temporal element of human friendship.[12]

Finally, Aelred, like all the authors of the heroic age of Cistercian literature, found "nothing could totally seize his affections which was not sweetened with the honey of Jesus and salted with the salt of the Holy Scriptures."[13]

Years of daily contact with the Scriptures had made their language part of his nature, so that he, like most monks, thought and wrote in biblical words without conscious quotations. There are thus references and allusions to scriptural phrases on every page of the *Spiritual Friendship,* even though many of the references are not exact quotations. It was not necessary for Aelred to cite the Scriptures or to check his references; instead the phrases and examples came to his pen almost automatically, expressing a way of thought more than an authority to be cited.

Since there is very little abstract discussion of friendship in the Bible, Aelred could not find there a doctrine to combine or contrast with Cicero's. But the Scriptures do have both an elaborate doctrine of love, which Aelred had already discussed in the *Mirror of Charity*, and a fund of epigrams and examples of friendship which can be quarried from the Old Testament.

The examples of friendship, which are to be found primarily in the historical books, are not of the most conspicuous borrowings of material from the Scriptures. Aelred consistently replaced Cicero's examples drawn from classical history and mythology with material from biblical history. Not only are these biblical events more likely to be familiar to his readers,

12. Aelred, Spir amic 3:48-49.
13. *Ibid.* Prologue :5.

but they also have a warmth and immediate appeal which the heroes and gods of classical antiquity conspicuously lack.[14]

There are also a number of brief epigrams from the wisdom books of the Old Testament which are referred to in the *Spiritual Friendship*. In most cases these references are incidental, and are used to sharpen or emphasize a point rather than to establish a principle. Thus the verse from Proverbs, "A true friend is a friend forever," emphasizes Aelred's contention that friendship, as a virtue, is eternal.[15]

It is interesting to notice that in the *Spiritual Friendship* Aelred almost completely neglects the technique of allegorical interpretation which he used with such virtuosity in his sermons and the little tract "On Jesus at Twelve Years Old." The only exception is a brief passage based on a verse from the Song of Songs, a work so popular with Cistercian authors for the profundity of its mystical content as to be almost impossible to avoid.[16] Nevertheless, in deference to the rules of the philosophical genre in which he was writing, Aelred carefully abstained from mixing in the sort of allegorical material which would have been appropriate to a work of edification.

Aelred's use of the New Testament is equally pervasive, and equally subtle. The Gospel according to John, the Gospel of love *par excellence,* was one of Aelred's favorite subjects of meditation, as was St Paul's doctrine of God's free and unconditional love for men. Direct quotation from St Paul is relatively rare in the *Spiritual Friendship,* but St John provided Aelred with material for some of his most striking phrases, such as the celebrated epigram "God is friendship."[17]

But perhaps even more striking than Aelred's confident reworking of his sources is his independent sympathy with the humanistic tradition. There is no need to insist that the first

14. E. g. Aelred discusses the story of David and Jonathan twice: in 2:63, where he stresses the disinterested quality of spiritual friendship, and in 3:92-95, where he stresses the complete equality which must exist between friends.

15. Proverbs 17:17. Aelred, Spir amic 1:21.

16. Song 1:1; Aelred, Spir amic 2:21-27. Both St Bernard and William of St Thierry found this verse particularly full of allegorical significance in their commentaries on the Song of Songs.

17. Aelred, Spir amic 1:69-70.

half of the twelfth century was an age of "renaissance," or
to suggest that classical literature and values were cultivated
in the Schools of all Europe. The north of Britain, too, had its
own tradition of learning and had played a noble role in the
preservation of the classics during the dark days of the barbar-
ian invasions; especially in Durham that tradition had never
been forgotten. Aelred was very much a part of that tradition
of classical education, and it was a happy fusion of his own
personal needs and the opportunities of his tradition which
enabled him to create the Classical-Christian humanism of the
Spiritual Friendship.

Even in the style of the book the fusion of these two elements
is obvious. It is rather a commonplace to contrast the monastic
style, with its leisurely development and constant, half-
conscious reminiscence of Scripture, with the bare, technical
prose of the schoolmen. It is true that both in his sources and
his style Aelred is typically monastic.

His language is clear, simple, and generally closer to St
Jerome's Vulgate than to Cicero's public style. There is a restraint to his style, an avoidance of the merely rhetorical,
which is classical in the best sense. Although steeped in the
writings of St Augustine, only rarely did he employ the con-
ceits of late Roman rhetoric which St Augustine had taught
and used. In fact, when Peter of Blois re-wrote the *Spiritual
Friendship* at the beginning of the thirteenth century, one of
his major concerns was to embellish Aelred's classical simplicity with baroque ornament.[18]

Aelred's prose also lacks the supreme polish of St Bernard's
finished works. Traces survive of drafts for some of his sermons and portions of the *Spiritual Friendship*,[19] but Aelred
did not have the time or the inclination to revise and polish
as carefully as St Bernard. He persuades not by the massive

18. R. W. Southern, "Peter of Blois, a Twelfth Century Humanist? " *Medieval
Humanism* (New York, 1970), pp. 121-122.

19. Anselm Hoste, "The First Draft of Aelred of Rievaulx' *De spirituali amicitia,"
Sacris Erudiri* 10 (1958), 186-193. See also C. H. Talbot, *Sermones inediti beati
Aelredi abbatis Rievallensis,* Series Scriptorum S. Ordinis Cisterciensis 1 (Rome,
1952) pp. 8-9. A. Squire, "The Literary Evidence for the Preaching of Aelred of
Rievaulx," *Cîteaux* 11 (1960), 165-177.

display of authorities, nor by the brilliance of his style, but by "his intense sensibility to emotions shared in some degree by all civilized mankind, and by reason also of a vivid power of self expression. . . ."[20]

20. David Knowles, "The Humanism of the Twelfth Century," in *The Historian and Character* (Cambridge, England, 1963), p. 21.

AELRED IN THE TRADITION OF
MONASTIC FRIENDSHIP

IN AELRED'S *SPIRITUAL FRIENDSHIP* we have both the supreme achievement of monastic speculation on friendship and the high water mark of that tradition. As is often the case, the partial and scattered opinions of the theorists of friendship found their best developed and most profound statement at just the time when the winds of change began to set against the monastic reform movement and the intimacy of monastic life as a whole.

As has been pointed out, the earliest monastic authors had been ambivalent about the value of particular friendships in the monastic community. The dangers to the spiritual life of pseudo-friendships, leading to factions and the danger of sexual temptation, had led most authors to stress the exclusive desire for God at the expense of the emotional satisfactions of love of neighbors and friends. Thus when Cassian treated the subject of personal friendships in the *Conferences* the weight of the discussion fell on avoiding anger and distraction from the purity of the love of God, rather than on the spiritual advantages of love between brothers.[1]

The literature of the Carolingian revival of the religious life is equally focused away from the particular friendship of the cloister. Mother A. M. Fisk has collected citations from Alcuin to Walafrid Strabo, showing that reformers and missionaries of the ninth and tenth centuries were alive to the needs and advantages of friendship, and felt free to use the rhetoric of

1. John Cassian, *Conferences*, 16 in *Nicene and Post-Nicene Fathers, Series Two*, ed. P. Schaff, H. Wace (Grand Rapids, Michigan, 1955), pp. 450-460; (CS 31).

friendship.[2] In almost every case, however, the emphasis is on a rather conventional and formal friendship, imitated from late Roman models of politeness, rather than a true and deeply felt intimacy. This is not to say that Carolingian authors are insincere, but simply that they stress the obligations of mutual aid and kindliness rather than the union of souls in a relation of disinterested spiritual love.

It is only in the eleventh century at such centers of monastic revival as Bec that spiritual friendship in the cloister itself enters the monastic tradition. In the charming and childlike person of St Anselm of Canterbury we suddenly see the rhetoric of epistolary friendship fuse with the inarticulate friendships of monks to become genuine spiritual friendship. Anselm developed a spirituality of friendship as an aspect of pursuit of God both in letters written before leaving Bec for Canterbury, and in his beautiful "Prayer for friends."[3] Once occupied by more complex and troublesome affairs as primate of all England, he displays in his surviving letters a more reserved and formal tone.

The beginning of the twelfth century was marked by the proliferation of new orders of monks and canons whose fervor and enthusiasm went far beyond the respectable, if slightly tepid, monasticism common in older Benedictine houses. This new fire could not help but encourage and spread the devotion to spiritual friendship. St Bernard and William of St Thierry, while retaining the natural distrust of those pseudo-friendships which could be so destructive in communities where the temperature of the monastic life was not kept at a pitch of white hot fervor,[4] wrote vividly of spiritual friendship.[5] Their en-

---

2. Fisk, *Friends*, pp. 5/1 to 14/15.

3. *Ibid.* pp. 15/1-32. See also R. W. Southern, *St Anselm and his Biographer* (Cambridge, England, 1963), pp. 67-76. There is an English translation of Anselm's Oratio 18, "A Prayer for Friends," in *Monastic Studies* 3 (1965), 235-236.

4. St Bernard, "Sermo in Cantica Canticorum 24:3," in *Opera omnia*, ed. J. Leclercq *et al.* I (Rome, 1957), p. 153: *Conciliant inter se inimicissimas amicitias, et pari consentaneae malignitatis affectu celebratur odiosa collatio. Haud secus egere quondam Herodes et Pilatus, de quibus narrat Evangelium quia facti sunt amici in illa die, hoc est in die dominicae passionis.*

5. For the more positive aspects of their treatment of friendship see Fisk, *Friends*, pp. 16/1-17/23.

thusiasm refused to be satisfied with the dry prudence of earlier authors, and they boldly explored the most shocking metaphors of the Song of Songs to express the energy of their passionate love.

It is in this context that Aelred's *Spiritual Friendship* must be read. Aelred was never indiscriminate in his enthusiasm, nor imprudent in his optimism, but he had the confidence typical of the early Cistercians in the fervor of his audience. He did not hesitate to warn of the dangers and snares of false friendships, but clearly found the advantages of friendship for the truly spiritual man outweighed the dangers to the unconverted. Such fervor and purity of intention is rare enough in this world, however, and within a few years a decided reaction had set in. After Aelred's death his successor found it necessary to appeal to the pope for action against fugitive monks, clear evidence that even at Rievaulx the heights could be inhabited for only a brief hour.[6]

The monastic order as a whole suffered the same fate as Rievaulx. The greatest days of the Cistercians were over by the death of St Bernard in 1153,[7] though the prestige of the Order remained exemplary for several generations. Writings by monastic authors on spiritual friendship almost disappear. It is true that Aelred's work was copied many times, and surviving manuscripts are very widespread—copies still exist from France and the Low Countries as well as from all parts of England. His work seems, however, to have inspired no successors in the monastic tradition, either because it was found to be a completely adequate treatment of the subject, or because the subject was no longer regarded with the same favor.

Outside the immediate monastic milieu, the reaction against spiritual friendship was slower in coming. By the end of the fourteenth century there were at least four short versions of the *Spiritual Friendship* in existence, one of which had achieved

6. Walter Daniel, *Life*, p. 40n.

7. In 1152 the General Chapter began to be alarmed at the expansion of the order and decreed that no new abbeys were to be founded. Even the papacy began to suspect something was amiss by the time of Pope Alexander III. See J. Leclercq, "Epîtres d'Alexandre III sur les Cisterciens," *Revue Bénédictine* 64 (1954), 68-82.

the honor of being attributed to St Augustine.[8] The author-ship of most of these versions is unknown, although one may in fact be a draft from Aelred's own hand[9] and another is attributed in the manuscripts to Thomas of Frakaham, an English Austin Friar of the thirteenth century.[10] This partic-ular version, which combines portions of the *Mirror of Charity* and the *Spiritual Friendship,* achieved considerable popularity: six manuscripts survive from as far away as Spain.[11]

Even more popular than these versions, however, was the full scale plagiarism which Peter of Blois undertook at the begin-ing of the thirteenth century.[12] Peter's work, titled *Christian Friendship,* is a careful re-writing of Aelred's *Spiritual Friend-ship* and *Mirror of Charity.* Large portions follow Aelred so closely that it is possible to emend textual corruptions in Peter's work by comparison with Aelred's text. The major changes are the result of a considerable expansion of the text in the flowery rhetorical style popular with cultivated readers in the thirteenth century. Peter's text itself enjoyed a false attribution to Cassiodorus in a number of manuscripts,[13] add-ing one more author to the number of those who have been given posthumous credit for Aelred's labors.

Even in the lay world Aelred's *Spiritual Friendship* seems to have achieved considerable popularity. A translation of at least a part of the work seems to have been undertaken by

8. These versions and the present locations of copies are listed in A. Hoste, *Bibliotheca Aelrediana* (Steenbrugge, Belgium, 1962), pp. 69-73.

9. A. Hoste, "The first draft of Aelred of Rievaulx' *De spirituali amicitia,*" *Sacris Erudiri* 10 (1958), 186-193.

10. A. Hoste, "The Speculum Spiritualis Amicitiae, a 13th c. compilation by Thomas de Frakaham, of two treatises by Aelred of Rievaulx," *Studia Monastica* 3 (1961), 291-295.

11. *Ibid.* pp. 295-296.

12. For Peter's career and the place of his work on friendship, see R. W. Southern, "Peter of Blois: a Twelfth Century Humanist?" in *Medieval Humanism* (New York 1970), pp. 105-129. The text is in PL 207:871-958, and in a modern edition, ed. M. M. Davy, *Un traité de l'amour du XIIe siècle* (Paris, 1932). Peter's use of Aelred is analysed by E. Vansteenberghe, "Deux théoriciens de l'amitié au XIIe siècle: Pierre de Blois et Aelred de Riéval," *Revue des sciences religieuses* 12 (1932), 572-588.

13. E. Bickel, "Peter von Blois und Pseudo-Cassiodor *De amicitia,*" *Neues Archiv* 45 (1923), 223-234.

Jean de Meun, the author of the *Romance of the Rose,* though no trace of this version survives.[14]

After the thirteenth century the influence of the *Spiritual Friendship* becomes more difficult to uncover. Dom Anselm Hoste has suggested that Peter of Herentals, a fourteenth-century Praemonstatensian prior of Floreffe, was acquainted with the work, but after that date the traces of Aelred's influence are lost to our view.[15]

The late middle ages and the counter-reformation shared a distrust of the "particular friendship" which at times borders on the neurotic. Friendships of any sort were banned from the cloister and the most ordinary of personal contacts were viewed with deep suspicion. Only in the twentieth century has Aelred's work again received its share of popular attention. As modern moral theology has turned away from the abstract and defensive attitude of handbook scholasticism, and as modern religions have turned their attention to the social implications of the Christian life, there has been a revival of interest in Aelred and in the *Spiritual Friendship.*[16]

In the last few years Aelred's book has had two critical editions[17] and been translated into French, German, and Italian. It was translated into English by C. H. Talbot in 1942[18] but wartime emergencies gave this version a very limited circulation. An English version of passages from the work by Sr M. F. Jerome was published in 1948.[19] The present version is thus the first translation in English based on a fully critical text and available to the general public. It is to be hoped it will make Aelred's Christian humanism better known and more widely appreciated.

14. There is a bibliography in Hoste, *Bibliotheca Aelrediana,* p. 67.

15. "*Dialogus inter Aelredum et discipulum:* an Adaptation of Aelred of Rievaulx' *De spirituali amicitia,*" *Citeaux* 10 (1959), 268.

16. E. g. Columban Heaney, "Aelred of Rievaulx: his Relevance to the Post-Vatican II Age," in *The Cistercian Spirit,* ed. M. Basil Pennington, Cistercian Studies Series 3 (Spencer, Mass., 1970), pp. 166-189.

17. A good text and French translation are given by J. Dubois, *L'amitié spirituelle* (Paris-Bruges, 1948), and the most recent critical edition is by A. Hoste, in *Aelredi Rievallensis opera omnia,* I, Corpus christianorum continuatio medievalis (Turnhout, Belgium, 1971).

18. *Christian Friendship* (London, 1942).

19. *Of Spiritual Friendship* (Paterson, N. J., 1948).

EDITORS NOTE

The translation presented here was originally based on the edition of the *De spirituali amicitia* published by J. P. Migne in volume 195 of the *Patrologiae Latinae* and compared with the text found in the *Maxima Bibliotheca Veterum Patrum* and other sources (see Selected Bibliography). It has however been carefully edited and revised in the light of the critical edition prepared by Dom Anselm Hoste, which has been published in the Corpus Christianorum Series. The section numbers used here are taken from the critical edition as these will undoubtedly become standard for references to this work. The notes added to the text are mine and I must take full blame for any deficiencies in them. I wish to express my sincere gratitude to Sr Eugenia for her beautiful translation and for her patience while we awaited the preparation of the Introduction, and especially to Prof Douglas Roby for stepping in and promptly preparing his fine Introduction when he was called upon in the eleventh hour.

M. Basil Pennington OCSO

SPIRITUAL FRIENDSHIP

PROLOGUE

WHEN I WAS STILL JUST A LAD at school, and the charm of my companions pleased me very much, I gave my whole soul to affection and devoted myself to love amid the ways and vices with which that age is wont to be threatened, so that nothing seemed to me more sweet, nothing more agreeable, nothing more practical, than to love.[1] 2. And so, torn between conflicting loves and friendships, I was drawn now here, now there, and not knowing the law of true friendship, I was often deceived by its mere semblance. At length there came to my hands the treatise which Tullius wrote on friendship,[2] and it immediately appealed to

1 . Cf. Augustine, *Confessions* 2:2; 3:1: tr. J. G. Pilkington in *Basic Writings of St Augustine* (New York: Random House, 1948) pp. 20, 29. It is not surprising to find right at the beginning of this dialogue on friendship the marked influence of St Augustine for none of the Fathers had so great an influence on the thinking of Aelred as did the Doctor of Hippo, especially through his *Confessions*. Walter Daniel in his *Life of Ailred* tells us that when Aelred was dying he ordered to be brought to him a Psalter, the *Confessions* of Augustine, and a text of St John's Gospel, and told the assembled brethren: "Behold I have kept these by me in my little oratory and have delighted in them to the utmost as I sat alone there in times of leisure."–W. Daniel, *Life of Ailred,* tr. F. W. Powicke (New York: Nelson, 1950) p. 58. The very complete apparatus accompanying the critical edition of the *De spirituali amicitia* indicates on almost every line of this prologue some allusion to Augustine's *Confessions*. "To love and to be loved," in the inverse order to what we find here but as it is in Augustine, is used by Aelred also in his *Mirror of Charity,* 1:25 (Cistercian Fathers Series, 17).

2. The reference is to Marcus Tullius Cicero, *De amicitia* sometimes called *Laelius,* which was written around the year 44 BC. Aelred borrows frequently from Cicero in this study on friendship, sometimes quoting him verbatim and indicating the borrowings. Other times he does not indicate them. While a list of

45

me as being serviceable because of the depth of his ideas, and fascination because of the charm of his eloquence. 3. And though I saw myself unfitted for that type of friendship, still I was gratified that I had discovered a formula for friendship whereby I might check the vacillations of my loves and affections.

When, in truth, it pleased our good Lord to reprove the wanderer, to lift the fallen, and with his healing touch to cleanse the leper, abandoning all wordly hopes, I entered a monastery. 4. Immediately I gave my attention to the reading of holy books, whereas prior to that, my eye, dimmed by the carnal darkness to which it had been accustomed, had not even a surface acquaintance with them. From that time on, Sacred Scripture became more attractive and the little learning which I had acquired in the world grew insipid in comparison. The ideas I had gathered from Cicero's treatise on friendship kept recurring to my mind, and I was astonished that they no longer had for me their wonted savor.[3] 5. For now nothing which had not been sweetened by the honey of the most sweet name of Jesus, nothing which had not been seasoned with the salt of Sacred Scripture, drew my affection so entirely to itself.[4] Pondering over these thoughts again and

parallel passages could be drawn up, there are yet pronounced differences. Aelred is far more systematic in his study of friendship, yet there is a rich, warm, personal touch in his presentation. The examples he chooses, too, are quite different from those of Cicero, who uses figures in Roman political life where Aelred draws on the Scriptures. While for Cicero friendship was a social grace, for Aelred it is a means to Christian perfection. For a full study of Cicero's influence on Aelred see J. Dubois' edition: Aelred de Rievaulx: *L'Amitié Spirituelle* (Paris: Beyaert, 1948) pp. xlviii ff.

3. The experience that Aelred describes here is almost the exact opposite of that of Augustine in his earlier life as he describes it in the *Confessions*: AC 3:5, p. 33.

4. Cf. the reaction of St Augustine to Cicero's *Hortensius*: "In the ordinary course of study, I lighted upon a certain book of Cicero, whose language, though not his heart, almost all admire. This book of his contains an exhortation to philosphy, and is called *Hortensius*. This book in truth, changed my affections . . . and since at that time (as you, O Lighted of my heart, know) the words of the Apostle were unknown to me, I was delighted with that exhortation, in so far only as I was thereby stimulated, and enkindled, and inflamed to love, seek, obtain, hold, and embrace, not this or that sect, but wisdom itself, whatever it were; and this alone checked me thus ardent that the name of Christ was not in it."—*Confessions* 3:4, p. 32. Perhaps Aelred's thought here is more directly influ-

again, I began to ask myself whether they could perhaps have some support from Scripture.

6. Since however I had already read many things on friendship in the writings of the saints, desiring this spiritual friendship but not being able to attain it, I decided to write my own book on spiritual friendship and to draw up for myself rules for a chaste and holy love.

7. Now, then, we have divided the work into three books: in the first, we study the nature of friendship, its source or cause; in the second we propose its fruition and excellence; in the third, we explain, to the best of our ability, how and among whom it can be preserved unbroken even to the end.[5]

8. Now, should anyone draw profit from reading this treatise, let him give thanks to God and ask for Christ's mercy upon my sins. But if anyone deems what I have written superfluous or impractical, let him pardon my unhappy position whose occupations forced me to put limits on the thought I could give to this meditation.

---

enced by Bernard of Clairvaux: Cf. *On the Song of Songs,* 15:6; CF 4:110: "But that name of Jesus is more than light, it is also food. . . . Every food of the mind is dry if it is not dipped in that oil; it is tasteless if not seasoned by that salt. Write what you will; I shall not relish it unless it tells of Jesus. Talk or argue about what you will, I shall not relish it if you exclude the name of Jesus. Jesus to me is honey in the mouth, music in the ear, a song in the heart."

5. Aelred gives here a clear outline of his work which he faithfully follows.

BOOK ONE

THE ORIGIN OF FRIENDSHIP

AELRED. Here we are, you and I, and I hope a third, Christ, is in our midst.[1] There is no one now to disturb us; there is no one to break in upon our friendly chat, no man's prattle or noise of any kind will creep into this pleasant solitude. Come now, beloved, open your heart, and pour into these friendly ears whatsoever you will, and let us accept gracefully the boon of this place, time, and leisure.

2. Just a little while ago as I was sitting with the brethren, while all around were talking noisily, one questioning, another arguing—one advancing some point on Sacred Scripture, another information on vices, and yet another on virtue—you alone were silent. At times you would raise your head and make ready to say something, but just as quickly, as though your voice had been trapped in your throat, you would drop your head again and continue your silence. Then you would leave us for a while, and later return looking rather disheartened. I concluded from all this that you wanted to talk to me, but that you dreaded the crowd, and hoped to be alone with me.

3. *Ivo.*[2] That's it exactly, and I deeply appreciate your solicitude for your son. His state of mind and his desire have

1. In the opening sentence of the dialogue Aelred expresses succinctly the essence of Christian friendship, two men together with Christ as their bond.

2. Ivo is usually identified as a monk of Wardon in Bedforshire. He might have been sent there from Rievaulx sometime after 1135. Since Wardon was a foundation of Rievaulx, Aelred would have gone there at least once a year to make the regular visitation. It was at the request of Ivo (presumably the same person) that

been disclosed to you by none other than the Spirit of Love. And would that your Lordship would grant me this favor, that, as often as you visit your sons here, I may be permitted, at least once, to have you all to myself and to disclose to you the deep feelings of my heart without disturbance.

4. *Aelred.* Indeed, I shall do that, and gladly. For I am greatly pleased to see that you are not bent on empty and idle pursuits, but that you are always speaking of things useful and necessary for your progress. Speak freely, therefore, and entrust to your friend all your cares and thoughts, that you may both learn and teach, give and receive, pour out and drink in.

5. *Ivo.* I am certainly ready to learn, not to teach; not to give, but to receive; to drink in, not to pour out; as indeed my youth demands of me, inexperience compels, and my religious profession exhorts. But that I may not foolishly squander on these considerations the time that I need for other matters, I wish that you would teach me something about spiritual friendship, namely, its nature and value, its source and end, whether it can be cultivated among all, and, if not among all, then by whom; how it can be preserved unbroken, and without any disturbance of misunderstanding be brought to a holy end.

6. *Aelred.* I wonder why you think it proper to seek this information from me, since it is evident that there has been enough, and more, discussion on matters of this kind by ancient and excellent teachers; particularly since you spent your youth in studies of this sort, and have read Cicero's treatise, *On Friendship*, in which in a delightful style he treats at length all those matters which appear to pertain to friendship, and there he sets forth certain laws and precepts, so to speak, for friendship.

7. *Ivo.* That treatise is not altogether unknown to me. In fact, at one time I took great delight in it. But since I began to taste some of the sweetness from the honey comb of Holy Scripture,

---

Aelred wrote his *Jesus at the Age of Twelve.* See *The Works of Aelred of Rievaulx*, vol. I (Cistercian Fathers Series 2); also *Ailred of Rievaulx, Christian Friendship*, trans. H. Talbot (London: Catholic Book Club, 1942) p. 9: Dubois, *op. cit.* p. lxxiii.

and since the sweet name of Christ claimed my affection for itself, whatever I henceforth read or hear, though it be treated ever so subtly and eloquently, will have no relish or enlightenment for me, if it lacks the salt of the heavenly books and the flavoring of that most sweet name.[3] 8. Therefore, those things which have already been said, even though they are in harmony with reason, and other things which the utility of this discussion demands that we treat, I should like proved to me with the authority of the Scriptures. I should like also to be instructed more fully as to how the friendship which ought to exist among us begins in Christ, is preserved according to the Spirit of Christ, and how its end and fruition are referred to Christ. For it is evident that Tullius was unacquainted with the virtue of true friendship, since he was completely unaware of its beginning and end, Christ.

9. *Aelred.* I confess I have been won over, but, not knowing myself or the extent of my own ability, I am not going to teach you anything about these matters but rather to discuss them with you. For you yourself have opened the way for both of us, and have enkindled that brilliant light on the very threshold of our inquiry, which will not allow us to wander along unknown paths, but will lead us along the sure path to the certain goal of our proposed quest. 10. For what more sublime can be said of friendship, what more true, what more profitable, than that it ought to, and is proved to, begin in Christ, continue in Christ, and be perfected in Christ? Come now, tell me, what do you think ought to be our first consideration in this matter of friendship?

Ivo. In the first place, I think we should discuss the nature of friendship so as not to appear to be painting in emptiness, as we would, indeed, if we were unaware of the precise identity of that about which an ordered discussion on our part should proceed.

11. *Aelred.* But surely you are satisfied, as a starting point, with what Tullius says, are you not? "Friendship is mutual harmony in affairs human and divine coupled with benevolence and charity."[4]

3. See above Prologue, note 4, p. 46.
4. Amic 20.

12. *Ivo.* If that definition satisfies you, I agree that it satisfies me.

13. *Aelred.* In that case, those who have the same opinion, the same will, in matters human and divine, along with mutual benevolence and charity, have, we shall admit, reached the perfection of friendship.

14. *Ivo.* Why not? But still, I do not see what the pagan Cicero meant by the word "charity" and "benevolence."

15. *Aelred.* Perhaps for him the word "charity" expresses an affection of the heart, and the word "benevolence," carrying it out in deed. For mutual harmony itself in matters human and divine ought to be dear to the hearts of both, that is, attractive and precious;[5] and the carrying out of these works in actual practice ought to be both benevolent and pleasant.

16. *Ivo.* I grant that this definition pleases me adequately, except that I should think it applied equally to pagans and Jews, and even to bad Christians. However, I confess that I am convinced that true friendship cannot exist among those who live without Christ.

17. *Aelred.* What follows will make it sufficiently clear to us whether the definition contains too much or too little, so that it may either be rejected, or if, so to say sufficient and not over inclusive, be admitted. You can, however, get some idea of the nature of friendship from the definition, even though it should seem somewhat imperfect.

18. *Ivo.* Please, will I annoy you if I say that this definition does not satisfy me unless you unravel for me the meaning of the word itself?

19. *Aelred.* I shall be glad to comply with your wishes if only you will pardon my lack of knowledge and not force me to teach what I do not know. Now I think the word *amicus* [friend] comes from the word *amor* [love], and *amicitia* [friendship] from *amicus*.[6] For love is a certain "affection" of the rational soul whereby it seeks and eagerly strives after some object to possess it and enjoy it. Having attained its object through love, it enjoys it with a certain interior sweetness,

5. In Latin a connection is seen between the words *caritas* (charity) and *carus* (precious).
6. Amic 26.

embraces it, and preserves it. We have explained the affections and movements of love as clearly and carefully as we could in our *Mirror*[7] with which you are already familiar.

20. Furthermore, a friend is called a guardian of love or, as some would have it, a guardian of the spirit itself.[8] Since it is fitting that my friend be a guardian of our mutual love or the guardian of my own spirit so as to preserve all its secrets in faithful silence, let him, as far as he can, cure and endure such defects as he may observe in it; let him rejoice with his friend in his joys, and weep with him in his sorrows,[9] and feel as his own all that his friend experiences.

21. Friendship, therefore, is that virtue by which spirits are bound by ties of love and sweetness, and out of many are made one.[10] Even the philosophers of this world have ranked friendship not with things casual or transitory but with the virtues which are eternal.[11] Solomon in the *Book of Proverbs* appears to agree with them when he says: "He that is a friend loves at all times,"[12] manifestly declaring that friendship is eternal if it is true friendship; but, if it should ever cease to be, then it was not true friendship, even though it seemed to be so.

22. *Ivo.* Why is it, then, that we read about bitter enmities arising between the most devoted friends?[13]

23. *Aelred.* God-willing, we shall discuss that matter more amply in its own place.[14] Meantime remember this: he was

7. The *Speculum Caritatis, Mirror of Charity* (Cistercian Fathers Series 17), written by Aelred while he was still novice master of Ricvaulx at the command of his Father Immediate (as Cistercians are accustomed to call the abbot of the motherhouse of their abbey), Bernard of Clairvaux. The third book especially of this work treats of friendship.
8. Isidore, *Etymologiae,* 10-5.
9. Rom 12:15.
10. Amic 81, 92. Cf. Spec car 3:39. Bernard of Clairvaux, Letter 53 (PL 182:160); tr. B. S. James, *The Letters of Bernard of Clairvaux* (London: Burns Oates, 1953) Letter 56, p. 84.
11. See Amic 32.
12. Prov. 17:17. Aelred quotes this verse from Proverbs again in the Third Book, n. 63, where he teaches that the fidelity of a person should be tested before he is accepted into full friendship. There he includes the second portion of the text: "He that is a friend loves at all times and a brother is proved in distress."
13. Amic 34.
14. See below, 3:39ff.

never a friend who could offend him whom he at one time received into his friendship; on the other hand, that other has
not tasted the delights of true friendship who even when offended has ceased to love him whom he once cherished. For
"he that is a friend loves at all times."[15] 24. Although he be
accused unjustly, though he be injured, though he be cast in
the flames, though he be crucified, "he that is a friend loves
at all times."[16] Our Jerome speaks similarly: "A friendship
which can cease to be was never true friendship."[17]

25. *Ivo.* Since such perfection is .expected of true friendship, it is not surprising that those were so rare whom the
ancients commended as true friends. As Tullius says: "In so
many past ages, tradition extols scarcely three or four pairs of
friends."[18] But if in our day, that is, in this age of Christian-
ity, friends are so few, it seems to me that I am exerting
myself uselessly in striving after this virtue which I, terrified
by its admirable sublimity, now almost despair of ever acquiring.

26. *Aelred.* "Effort in great things," as someone has said,
"is itself great."[19] Hence it is the mark of a virtuous mind to
reflect continually upon sublime and noble thoughts, that it
may either attain the desired object or understand more clearly
and gain knowledge of what ought to be desired. Thus, too, he
must be supposed to have advanced not a little who has learned,
by a knowledge of virtue, how far he is from virtue itself.
27. Indeed, the Christian ought not to despair of acquiring
any virtue since daily the divine voice from the Gospel re-
echoes: "Ask, and you shall receive. . . ."[20] It is no wonder,
then, that pursuers of true virtue were rare among the pagans
since they did not know the Lord, the Dispenser of virtue,[21]
of whom it is written: "The Lord of hosts, he is the King of

15. Prov 17:17.
16. *Ibid.*
17. St Jerome, *Letters,* 3:6; PL 22:335.
18. Amic 15.
19. Cf. Julius Pomerius, *De vita contemplativa,* I, Prologue, 2 (PL 59:416),
taken from the Pseudo-Seneca, *Monita,* 97.
20. Mt 7:7; Jn 16:24.
21. Cf. *Leonine Sacramentary,* 1229; ed. Mohlberg, p. 156, 17.

glory."[22] 28. Indeed, through faith in him they were prepared to die for one another—I do not say three or four, but I offer you thousands of pairs of friends—although the ancients declared or imagined the devotion of Pylades and Orestes a great marvel.[23] Were they not, according to the definition of Tullius, strong in the virtue of true friendship, of whom it is written: "And the multitude of believers had but one heart and one soul; neither did anyone say that aught was his own, but all things were common unto them"?[24] 29. How could they fail to have complete agreement on all things divine and human with charity and benevolence,[25] seeing that they had but one heart and one soul? How many martyrs gave their lives for their brethren! How many spared neither cost, nor even physical torments! I am sure you have often read—and that not dry-eyed—about the girl of Antioch rescued from a house of ill-repute by a fine bit of strategy on the part of a certain soldier.[26] Sometime later he whom she had discovered as a guardian of her chastity in that house of ill-repute became her companion in martyrdom. 30. I might go on citing many examples of this kind, did not the danger of verboseness forbid, and their very abundance enjoin us to be silent. For Christ Jesus announced their coming. He spoke, and they were

22. Ps 23:10.
23. Orestes, the son of Agamenon, after the murder of his father was secretly taken to the home of his uncle Strophius. Here he was raised along with his cousin Pylades and a very deep bond of union and love grew up between these two cousins. Pylades helped Orestes to avenge the murder of his father and the two fled together. However, Orestes was condemned to death in the land of his exile. At this point Pylades proved the depth of his friendship by seeking to take the place of Orestes and die in his stead. Their friendship became proverbial, and they were even worshiped by the Scythians. It was Pacuvius who brought their legend into Latin literature. However Aelred probably knew it from Cicero (Amic 24) and Augustine (*Confessions* 4:6).
24. Acts 4:32.
25. Aelred is here repeating the definition of Cicero, adding however the significant adjective "complete."
26. St Ambrose, *On Virgins*, 2:4 (PL 16:224f.). Aelred repeats here what is evidently an error on the part of Ambrose. The reference seems undoubtedly to be to Theodora of Alexandria rather than of Antioch, whose story is related in the Martyrology (April 28th). Didyme is the "certain soldier." Actually he simply disguised himself as a soldier in order to save Theodora and for this paid the price of being beheaded.

multiplied above number.[27] "Greater love than this," he says, "no man has, that a man lay down his life for his friends."[28]

31. *Ivo.* Are we then to believe that there is no difference between charity and friendship?

32. *Aelred.* On the contrary, there is a vast difference; for divine authority approves that more are to be received into the bosom of charity than into the embrace of friendship. For we are compelled by the law of charity to receive in the embrace of love not only our friends but also our enemies.[29] But only those do we call friends to whom we can fearlessly entrust our heart and all its secrets; those, too, who, in turn, are bound to us by the same law of faith and security.

33. *Ivo.* How many persons leading a worldly existence and acting as partners in some form of vice, are united by a similar pact and find the bond of even that sort of friendship to be more pleasant and sweet than all the delights of this world! 34. I hope that you will not find it burdensome to isolate, as it were, from the company of so many types of friendship that one which we think should be called "spiritual" to distinguish it from the others with which it is to some extent bound up and confused and which accost and clamor for the attention of those who seek and long for it. For by contrasting them you would make spiritual friendship better known to us and consequently more desirable, and thus more actively rouse and fire us to its acquisition.

35. *Aelred.* Falsely do they claim the illustrious name of friends among whom there exists a harmony of vices; since he who does not love is not a friend, but he does not love his fellow-man who loves iniquity. "For he that loves iniquity" does not love, but "hates his own soul."[30] Truly, he who does not love his own soul will not be able to love the soul of another.[31] 36. Thus it follows that they glory only in the name of friendship and are deceived by a distorted image and are

27. Ps 39:6.
28. Jn 15:13.
29. Mt 5:44; Lk 6:27f.
30. Ps 10:6.
31. Cf. Spec car 3:2.

not supported by truth. Yet, since such great joy is experienced in friendship which either lust defiles, avarice dishonors, or luxury pollutes, we may infer how much sweetness that friendship possesses which, in proportion as it is nobler, is the more secure; purer, it is the more pleasing; freer, it is the more happy. 37. Let us allow that, because of some similarity in feelings, those friendships which are not true, be, nevertheless, called friendships, provided, however, they are judiciously distinguished from that friendship which is spiritual and therefore true. 38. Hence let one kind of friendship be called carnal, another worldly, and another spiritual. The carnal springs from mutual harmony in vice; the worldly is enkindled by the hope of gain; and the spiritual is cemented by similarity of life, morals, and pursuits among the just.[32]

39. The real beginning of carnal friendship proceeds from an affection which like a harlot directs its step after every passer-by,[33] following its own lustful ears and eyes in every direction.[34] By means of the avenues of these senses it brings into the mind itself images of beautiful bodies or voluptuous objects. To enjoy these as he pleases the carnal man thinks is blessedness, but to enjoy them without an associate he considers less delightful. 40. Then by gesture, nod, words, compliance, spirit is captivated by spirit, and one is inflamed by the other, and they are kindled to form a sinful bond, so that, after they have entered upon such a deplorable pact, the one will do or suffer any crime or sacrilege whatsoever for the sake of the other. They consider nothing sweeter than this type of friendship, they judge nothing more equable, believing community of like and dislike[35] to be imposed upon them by the laws of friendship. 41. And so, this sort of friendship

32. Cf. Cassian, *Conferences,* 16:2 (Cistercian Studies Series 31).

33. Cf. Ezek 16:25 and Jerome's commentary on this: *Commentary on Ezekiel,* 4:16 (PL 25:138).

34. Num 15:39.

35. *Idem velle et idem nolle*—this is a proverbial saying which Sallust places in the mouth of Cataline as he urges his fellow conspirators in the name of friendship to join him in revolt; *Cataline* 20:4; tr. J. Watson, *Sallust, Flores and Vellius Paterculus* (New York: Harper, 1885) p. 25.

is undertaken without deliberation, is tested by no act of judgment, is in no wise governed by reason; but through the violence of affection is carried away through divers paths, observing no limit, caring naught for uprightness, foreseeing neither gains nor losses, but advancing toward everything heedlessly, indiscriminately, lightly and immoderately. For that reason, goaded on, as if by furies, it is consumed by its own self, or is dissolved with the same levity with which it was originally fashioned.

42. But worldly friendship, which is born of a desire for temporal advantage or possessions, is always full of deceit and intrigue; it contains nothing certain, nothing constant, nothing secure; for, to be sure, it ever changes with fortune and follows the purse.[36] 43. Hence it is written: "He is a fair-weather friend, and he will not abide in the day of your trouble."[37] Take away his hope of profit, and immediately he will cease to be a friend. This type of friendship the following lines very aptly deride:

A friend, not of the man, but of his purse is he,
Held fast by fortune fair, by evil made to flee.[38]

44. And yet, the beginning of this vicious friendship leads many individuals to a certain degree of true friendship: those, namely, who at first enter into a compact of friendship in the hope of common profit while they cherish in themselves faith in baneful riches, and who, in so far as human affairs are concerned, reach an acme of pleasing mutual agreement. But a friendship ought in no wise be called true which is begun and preserved for the sake of some temporal advantage.

45. For spiritual friendship, which we call true, should be desired, not for consideration of any worldly advantage or for any extrinsic cause, but from the dignity of its own nature and the feelings of the human heart, so that its fruition and reward is nothing other than itself.[39] 46. Whence the Lord in

---

36. Cf. Jerome, *Adv. Rufinum,* 1:17 (PL 23:430).

37. Sir 6:8.

38. No one seems to have been able yet to trace the source of this verse. Hoste (Spir amic, p. 176), Dubois (p. 29), Talbot (p. 135) all confess their ignorance as to the source.

39. Amic 31. Cf. Bernard of Clairvaux, *On the Song of Songs,* Sermon 83:4, OB 2:301; CF 40: "Love requires no other cause but itself, nor does it command a reward. Its reward is its enjoyment."

the Gospel says: "I have appointed you that you should go, and should bring forth fruit,"[40] that is, that you should love one another. For true friendship advances by perfecting itself, and the fruit is derived from feeling the sweetness of that perfection. And so spiritual friendship among the just is born of a similarity in life, morals, and pursuits, that is, it is a mutual conformity in matters human and divine united with benevolence and charity.[41]

47. Indeed, this definition seems to me to be adequate for representing friendship. If, however, "charity" is, according to our way of thinking, named in the sense that friendship excludes every vice, then "benevolence" expresses the feeling to love which is pleasantly roused interiorly. 48. Where such friendship exists, there, indeed, is a community of likes and dislikes,[42] the more pleasant in proportion as it is more sincere, the more agreeable as it is more sacred; those who love in this way can will nothing that is unbecoming, and reject nothing that is expedient. 49. Surely, such friendship prudence directs, justice rules, fortitude guards, and temperance moderates.[43] But of these matters we shall speak in their place. Now, then, tell me whether you think enough has been said about the matter you first brought up, namely, the nature of friendship.

50. *Ivo.* Your explanation is certainly sufficient, and nothing else suggests itself to me for further inquiry. But before we go on to other things, I should like to know how friendship first originated among men. Was it by nature, by chance or by necessity of some kind? Or did it come into practice by some statute or law imposed upon the human race, and did practice then commend it to man?

51. *Aelred.* At first, as I see it, nature itself impressed upon the human soul a desire for friendship, then experience in-

40. Jn 15:16f.
41. Amic 8,65. Cf. Conf. 16:3: "There is friendship which is constant and indissoluble, which is formed neither . . . in gifts received, nor in partnership in business, nor by instinct of nature, but which is cemented by likeness of manners or by the possession of the same virtues." SCh 54:224, CS 31. See also Chapter 5, *ibid.*
42. See above, note 35.
43. In his treatise on *Jesus at the Age of Twelve,* 20 (CF 2:27), Aelred brings out that the four cardinal virtues which he mentions here are nothing more than charity exercised in different circumstances. Therefore true friendship is simply friendship which is animated by charity.

creased that desire, and finally the sanction of the law con-
firmed it.[44] For God, supremely powerful and supremely good,
is sufficient good unto himself, since his good, his joy, his
glory, his happiness, is himself.[45] 52. Nor is there anything
outside himself which he needs, neither man, nor angel, nor
heaven, nor earth, nor anything which these contain. To him
every creature proclaims: "You are my God, for you have no
need of my goods."[46] Not only is he sufficient unto himself,
but he is himself the sufficiency of all things: giving simple
being to some, sensation to other, and wisdom over and above
these to still others, himself the Cause of all being, the Life of
all sensation, the Wisdom of all intelligence. 53. And thus
Sovereign Nature has established all natures, has arranged all
things in their places, and has discreetly distributed all things
in their own times. He has willed, moreover, for so his eternal
reason has directed, that peace encompass all his creatures and
society unite them; and thus all creatures obtain from him,
who is supremely and purely one, some trace of that unity.
For that reason he has left no type of beings alone, but out of
many has drawn them together by means of a certain society.

54. Suppose we begin with inanimate creation—what soil or
what river produces one single stone of one kind? Or what
forest bears but a single tree of a single kind? And so even in
inanimate nature a certain love of companionship, so to speak,
is apparent, since none of these exists alone but everything
is created and thrives in a certain society with its own kind.

And surely in animate life who can easily describe how
clear the picture of friendship is, and the image of society and
love?[47] 55. And though in all other respects animals are rated
irrational, yet they imitate man in this regard to such an
extent that we almost believe they act with reason. How they
run after one another, play with one another, so express and
betray their love by sound and movement, so eagerly and hap-

44. Amic 27.
45. Spec car 1:2.
46. Ps 15:2.
47. Amic 81.

pily do they enjoy their mutual company, that they seem to prize nothing else so much as they do whatever pertains to friendship.[48]

56. For the angels too divine Wisdom provided, in that he created not one but many. Among them pleasant companionship and delightful love created the same will, the same desire. Assuredly, since one seemed to be superior, the other inferior, there would have been occasion for envy,[49] had not the charity of friendship prevented it. Their multitude thus excluded solitude, and the bond of charity among many increased their mutual happiness.

57. Finally, when God created man, in order to commend more highly the good of society, he said: "It is not good for man to be alone: let us make him a helper like unto himself."[50] It was from no similar, nor even from the same, material that divine Might formed this help mate, but as a clearer inspiration to charity and friendship he produced the woman from the very substance of the man.[51] How beautiful it is that the second human being was taken from the side of the first, so that nature might teach that human beings are equal and, as it were, collateral, and that there is in human affairs neither a superior nor an inferior, a characteristic of true friendship. 58. Hence, nature from the very beginning implanted the desire for friendship and charity in the heart of man, a desire which an inner sense of affection soon increased with a taste of sweetness. But after the fall of the first man, when with the cooling of charity concupiscence made secret inroads and caused private good to take precedence over the common weal, it corrupted the splendor of friendship and charity through avarice and envy, introducing contentions, emulations, hates and suspicions because the morals of men had been corrupted. 59. From that time the good distinguished between charity and friendship, observing that love ought to be extend-

48. Amic 81. Cf. Conf. 16:2.
49. Amic 69, 71. Cf. Bernard of Clairvaux, *On the Song of Songs,* Sermon 59:2 (CF 31). See below, no. 57.
50. Gen 2:18.
51. Gen 2:21f.

ed even to the hostile and perverse, while no union of will
and ideas can exist between the good and wicked. And so
friendship which, like charity, was first preserved among all by
all, remained according to the natural law among the few
good. They saw the sacred laws of faith and society violated
by many and bound themselves together by a closer bond of
love and friendship. In the midst of the evils which they saw
and felt, they rested in the joy of mutual charity. 60. But in
those in whom wickedness obliterated every feeling for virtue,
reason, which could not be extinguished in them, left the
inclination toward friendship and society, so that without
companionship riches could hold no charm for the greedy, nor
glory for the ambitious, nor pleasure for the sensuous man.
There are compacts—even sworn bonds—of union among the
wicked which ought to be abhorred. These, clothed with the
beautiful name of friendship, ought to have been distinguished
from true friendship by law and precept, so that when true
friendship was sought, one might not incautiously be ensnared
among those other friendships because of some slight resemblance. 61. Thus friendship, which nature has brought into
being and practice has strengthened, has by the power of law
been regulated. It is evident, then, that friendship is natural,
like virtue, wisdom, and the like, which should be sought after
and preserved for their own sake as natural goods. Everyone
that possesses them makes good use of them, and no one
entirely abuses them.[52]

62. *Ivo.* May I ask, do not many people abuse wisdom?
Those, I mean, who desire to please men through it, or take
pride in themselves by reason of the wisdom placed in them
or certainly those who consider it a thing that can be sold, just
as they imagine there is a source of revenue in piety.[53]

63. *Aelred.* Our Augustine should satisfy you on that point.
Here are his words: "He who pleases himself, pleases a foolish
man, because, to be sure, he is foolish who pleases himself."[54]
But the man who is foolish is not wise; and he who is not
wise is not wise because he does not possess wisdom. How

52. St Augustine, *On Free Will,* 2:19.
53. St Augustine, Sermon 47:9ff. (PL 38:303).
54. Cf. St Bernard, SC 36:3; OB 2:5-6, CF 7.

then does he abuse wisdom who does not even possess it? And so proud chastity is no virtue, because pride itself, which is a vice, makes conformable to itself that which was considered a virtue. Therefore, it is not a virtue, but a vice.

64. *Ivo.* But I tell you, with your forbearance, that it does not seem consistent to me to join wisdom to friendship, since there is no comparison between the two.

65. *Aelred.* In spite of the fact that they are not coequal, very often lesser things are linked with greater, good with better, weaker with stronger. This is particularly true in the case of virtues. Although they vary by reason of a difference in degree, still they are close to one another by reason of similarity. Thus widowhood is near to virginity, conjugal chastity to widowhood. Although there is a great difference between these individual virtues, there is, nevertheless, a conformity in this, that they are virtues. 66. Now, then, conjugal chastity does not fail to be a virtue for the reason that widowhood is superior in continency. And whereas holy virginity is preferred to both, it does not thereby take away the excellence of the others. And yet, if you consider carefully what has been said about friendship, you will find it so close to, even replete with, wisdom, that I might almost say friendship is nothing else but wisdom.

67. *Ivo.* I am amazed, I admit, but I do not think that I can easily be convinced of your view.

68. *Aelred.* Have you forgotten that Scripture says: "He that is a friend loves at all times"?[55] Our Jerome also, as you recall, says: "Friendship which can end was never true friendship."[56] That friendship cannot even endure without charity has been more than adequately established. Since then in friendship eternity blossoms, truth shines forth, and charity grows sweet, consider whether you ought to separate the name of wisdom from these three.

69. *Ivo.* What does this all add up to? Shall I say of friendship what John, the friend of Jesus, says of charity: "God is friendship"?[57]

55. Prov 17:17.
56. Jerome, Letter 3:6; PL 22:335.
57. Cf. 1 Jn 4:16.

70. *Aelred.* That would be unusual, to be sure, nor does it have the sanction of the Scriptures. But still what is true of charity, I surely do not hesitate to grant to friendship, since "he that abides in friendship, abides in God, and God in him."[58] That we shall see more clearly when we begin to discuss its fruition and utility. Now if we have said enough on the nature of friendship in view of the simplicity of our poor wit, let us reserve for another time the other points you proposed for solution.

71. *Ivo.* I admit that my eagerness finds such a delay quite annoying, but it is necessary since not only is it time for the evening meal, from which no one may be absent, but, in addition, there are the burdensome demands of the other religious who have a right to your care.

58. *Ibid.*

BOOK TWO

THE FRUITION AND EXCELLENCE
OF FRIENDSHIP

AELRED. Come here now, brother, and tell me why you were sitting all alone a little while ago at some distance from us, when I was dealing with material affairs with those men of the flesh. There you were, turning your eyes now this way, now that; then you would rub your forehead with your hand; presently you would run your fingers through your hair;[1] again, frowning angrily, you would, with all sorts of faces, complain that something quite apart from your own desires had happened to you.

2. *Walter.* You have described the situation perfectly. For who could preserve his patience through a whole day seeing those agents of Pharaoh[2] getting your full attention, while we, to whom you are particularly indebted, were not able to gain even so much as a word with you?

3. *Aelred.* But we must show kindness to such people, too, for either we expect benefits from them or we fear their enmity. But since the doors have finally been closed upon them, solitude is the more gratifying to me now, in proportion

---

1. C. H. Talbot has an interesting note in regards to this "hair": "This seems to imply that Walter, though a monk, had no monastic tonsure. But during the first century of their existence, the Cistercians shaved tonsure and beard only seven times a year. This would allow Walter plenty of scope. In 1191 the number of shaving days was raised to nine, and in 1257 to twelve, reaching in 1293 twenty-five or six. This was a sign of relaxation frowned upon by the authorities, especially as the Dominicans, who lectured in the universities and who, presumably, would have to conform to the conventions of polite society, only shaved once every three weeks."—*op. cit.*, p. 138.
2. An allusion to Ex 5:14 which Aelred also uses in Spec car 1:18.

as that preceding disturbance was distressing. You know, "the best appetizer is hunger"[3]; and neither honey nor any other spice gives such relish to wine as a strong thirst does to water. And so perhaps this conference of ours, like spiritual food and drink, will be more enjoyable to you because of the intense longing preceding it. Come now, and do not delay proposing to me what you were preparing to unravel from your troubled heart a little while ago.

4. *Walter.* I shall, indeed; for it I be minded to make excuses because of the time, I shall be making even shorter the brief period they have left us. Tell me now, please, has it escaped your mind, or do you still remember the conversation which, once upon a time, you and your friend Ivo had on spiritual friendship? Do you recall what questions he proposed to you, how far you advanced in the explanation of these, and what you set down in writing upon the same points?

5. *Aelred.* Indeed, the fond memory of my beloved Ivo, yes, his constant love and affection are, in fact, always so fresh to my mind, that, though he has gone from this life in body, yet to my spirit he seems never to have died at all. For there he is ever with me,[4] there his pious countenance inspires me, there his charming eyes smile upon me, there his happy words have such relish for me, that either I seem to have gone to a better land with him or he seems still to be dwelling with me here upon earth. But you know that very many years have passed since we lost that bit of paper on which I had written his questions and my answers on spiritual friendship.

6. *Walter.* The facts do not escape me, but to be candid, all my eagerness and impatience arises from the fact that I have heard from certain individuals that this very paper was found and handed over to you three days ago. Please, show it to your son, for my spirit will not rest until I have reviewed the whole discussion and see what is still wanting in it, and then present to your fatherly examination for rejection or acceptance or

3. An ancient proverb which can be found, for example, in Xenophon, *Memorables,* 1, 3, 5: see Marbodus. *Prouerb.* (PL 171:1736); H. Walther, *Prouerbia Sententiaque Latinitatis Medii Aeui,* vol. 1 (Göttingen, 1936) p. 356.
4. Cf. Amic 102.

explanation whatever my own mind or secret inspiration suggest to me as matters requiring discussion.

7. *Aelred.* I shall comply with your wishes, but I desire that you alone should read what is written on it, and that it be not brought to public attention.[5] For I may, perhaps, decide that some points are to be omitted, some added, and, surely, many to be corrected.

* * * * *

8. *Walter.* Look, here I am, all ears to take in every word, the more avidly so since what I have read on friendship has so pleasant a taste. Since, therefore, I have read this excellent discussion on the nature of friendship, I should like to have you tell me what practical advantages it procures for those who cultivate it. For though it is a matter of such moment, as you seem to have thoroughly proved by means of unassailable arguments, yet it is only when its purpose and benefit are understood that it will be sought after with genuine ardor.

9. *Aelred.* I do not presume that I can explain it in a manner befitting the dignity of so signal a good, since in human affairs nothing more sacred is striven for, nothing more useful is sought after, nothing more difficult is discovered, nothing more sweet experienced, and nothing more profitable possessed. For friendship bears fruit in this life and in the next.[6]

10. It manifests all the virtues by its own charms; it assails vices by its own virtue; it tempers adversity and moderates prosperity. As a result, scarcely any happiness whatever can exist among mankind without friendship,[7] and a man is to be compared to a beast if he has no one to rejoice with him in adversity, no one to whom to unburden his mind if any annoyance crosses his path or with whom to share some un-

5. There is question here of an advisory reading prior to publication. See J. Leclercq, *Aspects litteraires de l'oeuvre de saint Bernard,* in *Cahiers de Civilis. Mediév.* 1 (1958) pp. 425-450. There we find the added injunction: "and do not give it to anyone to copy."—*Epistolae ad Seuerinum de caritate,* ed. G. Dumeige (Paris, 1955).

6. 1 Tim 4:8.

7. Amic 86. Cf. Bernard of Clairvaux, *Occasional Sermons I* 10:2; OB 6-1: 122-123; CF 46.

usually sublime or illuminating inspiration.[8] 11. "Woe to him that is alone, for when he falls, he has none to lift him up."[9] He is entirely alone who is without a friend.

But what happiness, what security, what joy to have someone to whom you dare to speak on terms of equality as to another self;[10] one to whom you need have no fear to confess your failings; one to whom you can unblushingly make known what progress you have made in the spiritual life; one to whom you can entrust all the secrets of your heart and before whom you can place all your plans! What, therefore, is more pleasant than so to unite to oneself the spirit of another and of two to form one, that no boasting is thereafter to be feared, no suspicion to be dreaded, no correction of one by the other to cause pain, no praise on the part of one to bring a charge of adulation from the other. 12. "A friend," says the Wise Man, "is the medicine of life."[11] Excellent, indeed, is that saying. For medicine is not more powerful or more efficacious for our wounds in all our temporal needs than the possession of a friend who meets every misfortune joyfully, so that, as the Apostle says, shoulder to shoulder, they bear one another's burdens.[12] Even more—each one carries his own injuries even more lightly than that of his friend. 13. Friendship, therefore, heightens the joys of prosperity and mitigates the sorrows of adversity by dividing and sharing them.[13] Hence, the best medicine in life is a friend. Even the philosophers took pleasure in the thought: not even water, nor the sun, nor fire do we use in more instances than a friend.[14] In every action, in every pursuit, in certainty, in doubt, in every event and fortune of whatever sort, in private and in public, in every deliberation, at home and abroad, everywhere friendship is found to be appreciated, a friend a necessity, a friend's service a thing of utility. "Wherefore, friends," says Tullius, "though absent are

8. Eccles 4:10. Cf. Spec car, 2:39. See also St Ambrose, *Duties* 3:131, p. 88.
9. Eccles 4:10.
10. Amic 22.
11. Sir 6:16.
12. St Paul:Gal 6:2.
13. Amic 22.
14. *Ibid.*

present, though poor are rich, though weak are strong, and—
what seems stranger still—though dead are alive.[15] 14. And
so it is that the rich prize friendship as their glory, the exiles
as their native land, the poor as their wealth, the sick as their
medicine, the dead as their life, the healthy as their charm, the
weak as their strength and the strong as their prize. So great
are the distinction, memory, praise and affection that accom-
pany friends that their lives are adjudged worthy of praise and
their death rated as precious.[16] And, a thing even more excellent than all these considerations, friendship is a stage border-
ing upon that perfection which consists in the love and knowledge of God, so that man from being a friend of his fellow-
man becomes the friend of God, according to the words of
the Savior in the Gospel: "I will not now call you servants,
but my friends."[17]

15. *Walter.* I confess your words have so moved me and so
enkindled my soul to a burning desire for friendship, that I
believe I am not even alive as long as I am deprived of the
manifold benefits of this great good. But what you said last,
the statement which aroused me so completely and almost
carried me away from all earthly things, I desire to hear
developed more fully, namely, that among the stages leading
to perfection friendship is the highest.

16. But see, here comes our friend Gratian, and quite op-
portunely. I might rightly call him friendship's child for he
spends all his energy in seeking to be loved and to love.[18] It is
opportune he came along, since he might be too eager for
friendship and be deceived by its mere semblance, mistake
the counterfeit for the true, the imaginary for the real, the
carnal for the spiritual.

17. *Gratian.*[19] I thank you for your courtesy, brother. One

15. Amic 23. Cf. Jerome, Ep 8:1; Bernard of Clairvaux, Ep 53; BLJ 56, p. 84;
Ep 65:2; BLJ 68, pp. 92ff.
16. Amic 23.
17. Jn 15:15.
18. See above, Prologue, note 1, p. 45.
19. We have no historical information concerning this Gratian. Indeed, he might
well be a purely fictional character, although there is no objective reason to
postulate this either. See Dubois, *op. cit.,* p. lxxxv.

not invited but rather boldly imposing himself, you grant a place at this spiritual banquet. But if you thought that I should be called friendship's child in earnest and not in jest, I should have been sent for at the beginning of this talk, and then I would not have had to lay aside due modesty and make a display of my eagerness. Nevertheless, Father, continue where you began, and for my sake set something on the table, so that, if I cannot be satiated as he is (for after consuming I know not how many courses, he summons me now to the remnants of the banquet of which he has grown disdainful), I may at least be able to be refreshed a little.

18. *Aelred.* You need have no fear, son, since matters of such importance still remain to be said on the good of friendship that, if some wise person were to carry them through to the end, you would think we had thus far said nothing. Nevertheless, turn your attention briefly to the manner in which friendship is, so to say, a stage toward the love and knowledge of God. Indeed, in friendship there is nothing dishonorable, nothing deceptive, nothing feigned; whatever there is, is holy, voluntary, and true.[20] And this itself is also a characteristic of charity.[21] 19. In this, truly, friendship shines forth with a special right of its own, that among those who are bound by the tie of friendship all joys, all security, all sweetness, all charms are experienced. Therefore, in the perfection of charity we love very many who are a source of burden and grief to us, for whose interest we concern ourselves honorably, not with hypocrisy or dissimulation, but sincerely and voluntarily, but yet we do not admit these to the intimacy of our friendship. 20. And so in friendship are joined honor and charm, truth and joy, sweetness and good-will, affection and action. And all these take their beginning from Christ, advance through Christ, and are perfected in Christ. Therefore, not too steep or unnatural does the ascent appear from Christ, as the inspiration of the love by which we love our friend, to Christ giving himself to us as our Friend for us to love, so that charm may follow upon charm, sweetness upon sweetness and affection upon affection. 21. And thus, friend cleaving to friend in the

20. Amic 26.
21. Cf. 2 Cor 13.

spirit of Christ, is made with Christ but one heart and one soul,[22] and so mounting aloft through degrees of love to friendship with Christ, he is made one spirit with him in one kiss.[23] Aspiring to this kiss the saintly soul cries out: "Let him kiss me with the kiss of his mouth."[24]

22. Let us consider the character of that carnal kiss, so that we may pass from the carnal to the spiritual, from the human to the divine.[25] Man needs two elements to sustain life, food and air. Without food he can subsist for some time, but without air he cannot live even one hour. And so in order to live, we inhale air with our mouths and exhale it. And that very thing which we exhale or inhale we call breath. 23. Therefore, in a kiss two breaths meet, and are mingled, and are united. As a result, a certain sweetness of mind is born, which rouses and binds together the affection of those who embrace.[26]

22. Acts 4:32.

23. Cor 6:17. Unity of spirit, being made one spirit with Christ, is a common theme among the Cistercian Fathers. See for example, William of St Thierry, *On Contemplating God 7*, CF 3:47-48; *The Golden Epistle* 262-263; CF 12:95-96; Gilbert of Swineshead, *Sermons on the Song of Songs*, 32:8, PL 184-170; Aelred of Rievaulx, *A Rule of Life for a Recluse*, 20, CF 2:74. This unity of spirit whereby man is made to be one spirit with Christ is not of the ontological order or a unity of nature. It is rather a untiy of wills or unity in charity. Bernard of Clairvaux makes this clear in his *Seventy-first Sermon on the Song of Songs*, n. 6: "The Word is in the Father and the Father is in the Word. Therefore, the union between them is in all respects perfect, and the Father and the Word are entirely and truly one. In this way, the soul for whom 'it is good to adhere to God' must not consider herself perfectly united to him until she has perceived that he abides in her and she in him. Not that she can say, even then, that she is one with God in the same sense in which the Father and the Word are one, although the Apostle assures us that 'he who is joined to the Lord is one spirit.' Thus we have scriptural authority for the unity of spirit between God and the soul, but not for any unity of nature . . . no creature whatever, whether of earth or heaven, unless one has taken leave of his senses, will dare to assert the words of the Only Begotten and presume to say, 'I and the Father are one.' On the other hand . . . I should not feel the slightest hesitation in saying that I was one spirit with God if only I were convinced that I adhered to him like one of those who abide in them. . . . It is to this kind of union that the Apostle refers, I think, when he says, 'He who is joined to the Lord is one spirit.' "—OB 2:218, CF 40.

24. Song 1:1.

25. Cf. Aelred's *Second Sermon for the Feast of the Epiphany* (CF 23); Bernard of Clairvaux, *On the Song of Songs*, 3, 4, 8, 9 (CF 4); Occasional Sermons, 10, 87 (CF 46). Walter Daniel, *Centum Sententiae*, 45—ed. C. H. Talbot, in *Sacris Erudiri*, 11 (1960) p. 295f.

26. Cf. William of St Thierry, *Exposition on the Song of Songs*, 30f, CF 6:25-26; *Meditations*, 8:5, CF 3:142.

24. There is, then, a corporeal kiss, a spiritual kiss, and an intellectual kiss. The corporeal kiss is made by the impression of the lips; the spiritual kiss by the union of spirits; the intellectual kiss through the Spirit of God, by the infusion of grace.

Now the corporeal kiss ought not to be offered or received except for definite and worthy reasons: for example, as a sign of reconciliation, when they become friends who were previously at enmity with one another;[27] or as a mark of peace, as those who are about to communicate in church manifest by an external kiss their interior peace; or as a symbol of love, such as is permitted between bride and bridegroom or as is extended to and received from friends after a long absence; or as a sign of catholic unity, as is done when a guest is received. 25. But just as many people misuse water, fire, iron, food and air, which are natural goods, by employing them as instruments of their cruelty and lust, so, too, the perverse and lustful strive to give a relish to their shameful acts even with this good which the natural law has instituted to signify the things we have indicated, defiling this very kiss with such shame that thus to be kissed is nothing else than to be corrupted. How much such a kiss ought to be detested, abominated, shunned, resisted, every honorable person knows.

26. In the next place, the spiritual kiss is characteristically the kiss of friends who are bound by one law of friendship; for it is not made by contact of the mouth but by the affection of the heart;[28] not by a meeting of lips but by a mingling of spirits, by the purification of all things in the Spirit of God,[29] and, through his own participation, it emits a celestial savor. I would call this the kiss of Christ, yet he himself does not offer it from his own mouth, but from the mouth of another,[30] breathing upon his lovers that most sacred affection so that there seems to them to be, as it were, one spirit in many bodies. And they may say with the Prophet: "Behold how good and how pleasant it is for brethren to dwell together

27. Lk 23:12.
28. Spec car 1:34.
29. Cf. Pseudo-Ignatius, *Epist. ad Trallianos,* 13:3; ed. Funk, vol. 2, p. 113.
30. Cf. Quintillianus, *Institutio* 11:1.

in unity."[31] 27. The soul, therefore, accustomed to this kiss and not doubting that all this sweetness comes from Christ, as if reflecting within itself and saying, "Oh, if only he himself had come!" sighs for the kiss of grace and with the greatest desire exclaims: "Let him kiss me with the kiss of his mouth."[32] So that now, after all earthly affections have been tempered, and all thoughts and desires which savor of the world have been quieted, the soul takes delight in the kiss of Christ alone and rests in his embrace, exulting and exclaiming: "His left hand is under my head and his right hand shall embrace me."[33]

28. *Gratian.* This type of friendship, as I see it, is not common, nor are we accustomed to dream of friendship as having such a character. I do not know what thought Walter has given it so far, but, as for me, I believed friendship was nothing else than so complete an identity of wills between two persons that the one would wish nothing which the other did not wish,[34] and that so great was the mutual harmony between both, in fortune good and evil, that neither life, nor wealth, nor honor, nothing whatsoever belonging to the one was denied to the other for his enjoyment and use according as he wished.

29. *Walter.* I remember having learned something quite different in the first dialogue where the very definition of friendship, set forth and explained, duly and ardently inspired me to a more profound contemplation of its fruit. As we have been sufficiently informed on this point, we are trying to set up for ourselves a definite limit as to how far friendship ought to go, since in this matter there is a difference of opinion among various individuals. Now there are some who think they ought to love their friends contrary to faith and honor, contrary to common or private good. Some judge that faith alone excepted, the rest should not be held back.[35] 30. Others believe that on behalf of a friend one ought to spurn money, reject honors, submit to enmities from those in high places,

31. Ps 132:1.
32. Song 1:1.
33. *Ibid.* 2:6.
34. See above, Part I, note 35, p. 59.
35. Amic 61.

and not even shun exile; that one should even expose oneself to what is dishonorable and vile, provided only one's native land is not the sufferer nor one's neighbor hurt. Again there are those who set up this as the goal of friendship, that each one will so conduct himself toward his friend as he would toward himself. 31. And some believe they satisfy the demands of friendship when they mutually repay their friend for every benefit of service.[36]

But from this discussion of ours, I am convinced that I ought not have faith in any of these theorists, and for that reason I should like you to set up a definite limit for friendship, particularly on account of Gratian here, that he may not, in accordance with his name, be so eager to be gracious that he recklessly become vicious.

32. *Gratian.* I sincerely appreciate your thoughtful concern for me; and if I were not hampered by my eagerness to hear, I should, perhaps, take my revenge on you now. But let us hear together what response he plans to give to your questioning.

33. *Aelred.* Christ himself set up a definite goal for friendship when he said: "Greater love than this no man hath, that a man lay down his life for his friends."[37] See how far love between friends should extend; namely, that they be willing to die for one another. Does that seem adequate to you?

34. *Gratian.* Since no greater friendship is possible, why should it not be adequate?

35. *Walter.* But if the wicked or pagans take such joy in the mutual harmony of evil and wickedness that they are willing to die for one another, shall we grant that they have reached the zenith of friendship?

36. *Aelred.* Heaven forbid, since friendship cannot exist among the wicked.

37. *Gratian.* Tell us, pray, among whom it can arise and be preserved?

38. *Aelred.* I shall tell you in a few words. It can begin among the good, progress among the better and be consum-

---

36. These two last opinions are recounted by Cicero, but he does not indicate their authorship: Amic 56.
37. Jn 15:13.

mated among the perfect.[38] For as long as any one delights in an evil thing from a desire of evil, as long as sensuality is more gratifying than purity, indiscretion than moderation, flattery than correction, how can it be right for such a one even to aspire to friendship, when it springs from an esteem for virtue?[39] It is difficult therefore, nay, impossible, for you to taste its beginnings, if you do not know the fountain from which it can spring. 39. For that love is shameful and unworthy of the name of friendship wherein anything foul is demanded of a friend; and this is precisely what one is forced to do, if, with vices in no wise dormant or subdued, he is either enticed or impelled to all sorts of illicit acts. Therefore, one ought to detest the opinion of those who think that one should act in behalf of a friend in a way detrimental to faith and uprightness. 40. For it is not excuse for sin, that you sin for the sake of a friend.

The first of men, Adam, would have done better had he charged his wife with presumption instead of complying with her request by eating the forbidden fruit.[40] And far better did the servants of King Saul preserve their loyalty to their master by withdrawing their hands from blood in violation of his command, than Doeg, the Edomite, who as minister of the royal cruelty killed with sacrilegious hands the priests of the Lord.[41] Jonadab, too, the friend of Ammon, would have acted more laudably in preventing the incest of his friend than by offering advice to aid him in obtaining his object.[42] 41. Nor does the virtue of friendship excuse the friends of Absalom, who, consenting to treason, bore arms against their native country.[43] But to come to these our own times, Otto, Cardinal of the Roman Church, certainly was far more blessed

---

38. Amic 18. Cf. John Cassian Conf, 16:3: "If then, you are desirous of lasting friendship, be diligent in cleansing your souls from all vice, and mortify your wills, that being united in the same desires and affections, you may attain to that peaceful state which David pronounces to be so pleasant and so happy: 'Behold how good and how pleasant it is for brethren to dwell together in unity.' "—SCh 54:226. "Hence the maxim of the Fathers: no friendship, no union, can be true except among persons solidly virtuous."—SCh 54:247, CS 31.

39. Amic 37, 40.
40. Gen 3:6.
41. 1 Sam 22:17f.
42. 2 Sam 13:3ff.
43. 2 Sam 15:12f.

in abandoning his close friend Guido than John was in cling-ing to his Octavian in so great a schism.[44] You see, therefore, that friendship cannot exist except among the good.[45]

42. *Gratian.* What, then, has friendship to do with us, who are not good?

43. *Aelred.* I am not cutting "good" so finely as do some who call no one "good" unless he is lacking no whit in per-fection.[46] We call a man "good" who, according to the limits of our mortality,[47] "living soberly and justly and godly in this world."[48] is resolved neither to ask others to do wrong nor to do wrong himself at another's request.[49] Among such, indeed, we do not doubt that friendship can spring up and that by such it can be perfected. 44. As for those who, apart from faith, danger to their fatherland, or unjust injury to an-other, put themselves at the disposal of the pleasure of their friends, I would say they are not so foolish as they are insane; sparing others, they do not see fit to spare themselves; and safe-guarding the honor of others they unhappily betray their own.[50]

45. *Walter.* I almost agree with the opinion of those who say that friendship should be avoided, on the ground that it is a compact full of solicitude and care, not devoid of fear, and even subject to many griefs.[51] For since it is enough and more

44. Octavian Maledetti, an anti-pope who took the name of Victor IV, was elected in 1159 at the time of the death of Adrian IV. He had the support of Frederick I against Alexander III, the true Pope. The Cistercians remained faithful to Alexander III. See J. Canivez, *Statuta Capitulorum Generalium Ordinis Cister-ciensis ab anno 1116 ad annum 1786*, vol. 1 (Louvain, 1933), p. 73. John of St Martin, a Cardinal Priest, had concurred in the election of Octavian. Octavian died on April 20, 1164. Cardinal Guido de Crene succeeded him and took the name of Pascal III. Otto was a Cardinal who belonged to the group supporting Guido. This passage is important for helping us date the writing of the *Spiritual Friendship*. See the Introduction in Dubois, *op. cit.*, p. xcii.

45. Amic 18.

46. *Ibid.* This is a reference to some of the ideas of the Stoics.

47. Cf. Amic 50; Bernard of Clairvaux, Ep 270-3; BLJ 340, p. 419.

48. Titus 2:12.

49. Amic 40.

50. Amic 39.

51. Walter here presents rather succinctly the position of the Stoics. See Seneca's *Letter to Lucilius*, 9:1; trans. R. M. Gummere, *The Epistles of Seneca*, vol. 1, Loeb Classical Series (New York: Putnam, 1925), p. 43.

than enough for anyone to bear his own burden,[52] they say a
man acts rashly in so tying himself to others, that he must
needs be involved in many cares and afflicted with many
evils. 46. Moreover, they think nothing is more difficult than
for friendship to abide even to the day of death, while on the
other hand it would be quite shameful for a friendship to be
formed and then turn into the opposite.[53] Therefore they
judge it safer so to love others as to be able to hate them at
will, and in so relaxed a manner to hold the reins of friendship that they may be tightened or loosened at will.[54]

47. *Gratian.* We have been laboring in vain, then, you in
speaking, we in listening, if we can so easily withhold ourselves
from the desire of friendship, the fruit of which is so holy, so
useful, so acceptable to God, and so near to perfection and
recommended to us in so many ways. Let us leave the opinion
you have spoken of to the man who wishes today's love to be
such that it may turn into hatred tomorrow; who wishes to
be the friend of all without trusting any; who praises today and
reviles tomorrow; who flatters today and criticizes tomorrow;
who today is prepared for kisses and tomorrow is ready for
reproaches. The love of such a man is acquired at a small
price, and at the slightest offense it disappears.

48. *Walter.* I used to think that doves lacked gall. But at
any rate tell us how the opinion of those individuals who
displease Gratian so much can be refuted.

49. *Aelred.* Tullius speaks beautifully on this point: "They
seem," he says, "to take the sun out of the world who take
friendship out of life, for we have nothing better from God,
nothing more pleasant."[55] What wisdom is there in despising
friendship so that you may avoid solicitude, be free from
cares, be devoid of fear?—as if any virtue can be acquired
or preserved without solicitude.[56] Take your own life—does

52. Amic 45.

53. Amic 59.

54. Amic 45. Here Aelred reproduces Cicero almost word for word and Cicero
in his turn is but translating Euripides, *Hippolytus,* 253ff, tr. A. Way, Loeb
Classical Series, vol. 4 (New York: Putnam, 1922), p. 181.

55. Amic 47. Where Aelred speaks of "God," Cicero speaks of "the immortal
gods."

56. Amic 48. Cf. Augustine, *The City of God,* 19:8.

prudence struggle against error, temperance against wantonness, justice against cunning, fortitude against cowardice, without any great anxiety on your part? 50. Who, I ask, among men, especially among the young, is able to preserve his purity or restrain his sensual appetite without very great grief or fear?

Paul must have been a fool, for he was unwilling to live without care and solicitude for others; but for the sake of charity which he believed to be the sovereign virtue, he was weak with the weak, on fire with the scandalized.[57] And too, great sorrow was his and continual grief of heart on behalf of his brethren in the flesh.[58] 51. Therefore he ought to have given up charity, assuredly under so many anxieties and griefs, now being "against labor" for those whom he had begotten;[59] now "cherishing as a nurse";[60] now as a master admonishing;[61] now fearing lest their minds be seduced from the faith;[62] now with much grief and many tears exhorting to penance;[63] now grieving over the impenitent.[64]

You see how those seek to take virtues out of the world who fear not to take solicitude, their associate, from our midst. 52. Was it to no purpose that Chusai, the Arachite, preserved with such great fidelity his friendship with David, that he preferred anxiety, and would rather share the griefs of his friend than relax amid the joys and honors of the parricide?[65] I would say that those men are beasts rather than human beings who declare that a man ought to live in such a way as to be to no one a source of consolation, to no one a source even of grief or burden; to take no delight in the good fortune of another, or impart to others no bitterness because of their own misfortune, caring to cherish no one and to be cherished by no one. 53. Heaven forbid that I should grant

57. 2 Cor 11:28f.
58. Rom 9:2f.
59. 1 Thess 2:7.
60. Col 1:28.
61. 2 Tim 2:25.
62. 2 Cor 11:3.
63. 2 Cor 2:4.
64. 2 Cor 12:21.
65. 2 Sam 16:15ff.; 17:5ff.

that they truly love anyone who think of friendship as a trade; for such with their lips only declare themselves friends when the hope of some temporal advantage favors them or when they try to make their friend an accomplice in some sort of base deed.[66]

54. *Walter.* Since, therefore, it is agreed that many are deceived by the mere semblance of friendship, tell us, pray, what sort of friendship we ought to avoid and what sort we ought to seek, cherish and preserve.

55. *Aelred.* Since we have said that friendship cannot endure except among the good, it is easy for you to see that no friendship which would be unbecoming to the good is acceptable.

56. *Gratian.* But perhaps we are not clear on the distinction between what is becoming and what is unbecoming.

57. *Aelred.* I shall comply with your wishes and state in a few words what friendships ought to be avoided should they present themselves to us. There is the puerile friendship begotten of an aimless and playful affection, directing its step after every passer-by without reason, without weight, without measure, without consideration of advantage or disadvantage. This type of friendship for a time affects one strongly, it draws one rather closely, and entices one rather flatteringly. But affection without reason is an animal movement, inclined to everything illicit, nay, unable to discern licit from illicit.[67] Moreover, although affection, for the most part, commonly precedes friendship yet it ought never be followed unless reason lead it, honor temper it, and justice rule it. 58. Hence, this friendship which we have styled puerile, because it is chiefly in children that feelings hold sway, ought, as a thing unfaithful, unstable, and always mixed with impure loves, to be guarded against in every way by those who take delight in the sweetness of spiritual friendship. We call it not friendship but friendship's poison since the proper bounds of love, which extend from soul to soul, can never be observed in it.

66. Amic 79. Cf. Conf 16:28: "It has also been shown by experience that friendships begun . . . without a desire for perfection, or for fulfilling the apostolic precept of charity, but for satisfying earthly love . . . cannot long preserve their unity unbroken."—SCh 54:246-247, CS 31.

67. Spec car 1:25.

Rather rising like a mist from the concupiscence of the flesh
it obscures and corrupts the true character of friendship, and
through neglect of the spirit it draws one to the desires of the
flesh.[68] 59. For that reason the beginnings of spiritual friendship ought to possess, first of all, purity of intention, the
direction of reason and the restraint of moderation; and thus
the very desire for such friendship, so sweet as it comes upon
us, will presently make friendship itself a delight to experience,
so that it will never cease to be properly ordered.[69]

Then there is the friendship which is based on a likeness in
evil. Of this type I refrain from speaking, since, as we have
said before, it is not to be considered even worthy of the name
of friendship

60. There is, besides, a friendship which the consideration
of some advantage excites and which many think ought to be
sought, encouraged and preserved for this reason.[70] But if we
admit this type, how many most worthy of all love shall we
exclude, those, namely, who, since they have nothing and possess nothing, offer, assuredly, no material gain or hope therefore
to anyone! 61. But if you include among "advantages,"
counsel in doubt, consolation in adversity, and other benefits
of like nature—these in any case, are to be expected from a
friend, but they ought to follow friendship, not precede it.
For he has not yet learned what friendship is who wishes any
reward other than itself.[71] Such a reward friendship will cer-

68. Cf. Augustine, *Confessions* 2:2, 3:1.

69. The experience of sweetness which is granted to those who begin to follow
the ways of virtue, and in this case spiritual friendship, is a characteristic note in
the spirituality described by the Cistercians.

70. While Cicero in his *De inventione,* 2:55, allowed for a type of friendship
based on such motivations as are expressed here, he later in Amic (25, 50) rejected this as not being true friendship and developed the line of thinking which
Aelred presents here. However in this instance Aelred is undoubtedly also influ-
enced by Augustine, Sermon 385:4 (PL 39:1692): "The love of friendship should
be gratuitous. You ought not to have or to love a friend for what he will give you.
If you love him for the reason that he will supply you with money or some other
temporal favor, you love the gift rather than him. Friends should be loved freely
for themselves and not for anything else."

71. Amic 30. Cf. Bernard of Clairvaux, *On the Song of Songs,* 83:5, OB 2:301,
CF 40; *On Loving God,* 7:17, OB 3:134, CF 13: "True love is its own fulfillment.
It has a reward, but it is the possession of the object it loves . . . true love asks no
reward, but deserves one."

tainly be for those cultivating it, when, wholly translated to God, it immerses in the divine contemplation those whom it has united. 62. For, although friendship, sure of its blessings, brings many great advantages, nevertheless we are certain that friendship does not proceed from the advantages but rather the advantages proceed from it.[72] Indeed, we do not believe that a friendship arose between those great men because of the benefits which Barzillai, the Gileadite, bestowed on David when he was fleeing from his parricide son, receiving him, taking care of him, counting him among his friends, but rather we do not doubt that such favor proceeded from friendship itself. For there is no one who thinks that the king was in need of that man previous to his friendship with him.[73] 63. Indeed, that he himself, a man of great wealth, hoped for no recompense from the king for his deeds one can clearly observe from the fact that when the king so generously offered him all the delights and riches of the state, he would not agree to take anything, preferring to be content with what he had.[74] Similarly, we know that the sacred bond of friendship between David and Jonathan, which was consecrated not through the hope of future advantage, but from the contemplation of virtue,[75] was very profitable for both. The life of the one was preserved by the ingenuity of the other but to his own benefit, in that his own posterity was thus preserved.[76] 64. Since, therefore, among the good, friendship always precedes and advantage follows, surely, it is not so much the benefit obtained through a friend that delights as the friend's love in itself.[77]

Now, then, whether we have said enough on the fruits of friendship or indicated clearly among which individuals it can begin, be preserved, and be perfected; whether, besides, we have plainly disclosed the flattering subserviency which is clothed with the false name of friendship, and whether also

72. Amic 30.
73. 2 Sam 17:27f. Compare this to what Cicero has to say (Amic 30) concerning Scipio and Lelius. See also Spec car 3:13.
74. 2 Sam 19:31ff.
75. Amic 30.
76. 1 Sam 19-20; 2 Sam 9.
77. Amic 51.

we have set forth the definite limits up to which love among friends ought to be extended: of all these questions you yourselves be the judges.

65. *Gratian.* I do not recall that this last point was sufficiently explained.

66. *Aelred.* But you remember, I think, that I refuted the opinion of those who establish the limits of friendship at agreement on vices and evil deeds; of those also, who think that one ought to go so far as to suffer exile and any form of dishonor, provided no harm is done to one's neighbor. 67. But I have also refuted the opinion of those who measure out their friendship with the yardstick of advantages anticipated. However, two of those forms of friendship which Walter proposed I did not consider even worthy of mention. For what can be more absurd than to extend friendship to the mere mutual repayment of one's friend through services and compliments, since all things ought to be in common among those who should indeed be of one mind and one soul?[78] How base this, too, would be, for anyone to regard his friend only in the same way he regards himself, since each ought to have a low opinion of himself and a high opinion of his friend!

68. Then, when we had completely disposed of these false ends of friendship, we thought that the true end ought to be set forth from the words of the Lord, who has taught that death itself in behalf of a friend should not be shunned. But in order that base individuals thus disposed and willing to die for one another might not be regarded as having reached the zenith of friendship, we further indicated among which persons friendship can arise and be perfected. Then we expressed the belief that those, who, on account of the many anxieties and cares which friendship entails, think it should for that reason be avoided, ought to be charged with absurdity. Finally, we explained as briefly as possible which friendships ought to be avoided by all good people.

69. It is clear, then, from this whole discussion, what the fixed and true limit of spiritual friendship is: namely, that

nothing ought to be denied to a friend, nothing ought to be refused for a friend, which is less than the very precious life of the body, which divine authority has taught should be laid down for a friend. Hence, since the life of the soul is of far greater excellence than that of the body, any action, we believe, should be altogether denied a friend which brings about the death of the soul, that is, sin, which separated God from the soul and the soul from life. But what limit ought to be preserved and what caution be maintained in those actions which one should perform for a friend, or tolerate in his behalf, this is not the time to decide.

70. *Gratian.* I admit that our friend Walter has benefited me not a little. In response to his questioning, you have summed up in a brief epilogue the principal points of the discussion, and have, so to speak, fixed them in the memory. And now, please tell us what limit should be preserved in serving one's friends, and what caution should be kept in mind.

71. *Aelred.* Both these and other matters pertaining to friendship remain to be discussed. But an hour has already passed, and these others who have just arrived are by their impatience, as you see, hustling me off to other business.

72. *Walter.* You may be sure I leave unwillingly. Tomorrow, indeed, when occasion presents itself, I intend to return. And let our friend Gratian see to it that he is on time tomorrow morning, that he may not accuse us of neglect, or we accuse him of tardiness.

BOOK THREE

THE CONDITIONS AND CHARACTERS
REQUISITE FOR UNBROKEN FRIENDSHIP

AELRED. Where have you come from and why have you
you come?

Gratian. Surely you know why I am here.

Aelred. Isn't Walter present?

Gratian. Let him see to that himself; surely he cannot accuse us of tardiness today.

Aelred. Do you want to follow up the questions which have been proposed?

Gratian. I have confidence in Walter, for I confess I do need his presence. He is quicker in grasping things, better at questioning, and has a better memory, also.

(Enter Walter)

Aelred. Did you hear that, Walter? Gratian is more friendly to you than you thought.

Walter. How could he fail to be my friend, since he is everybody's friend? But now that we are both here, mindful of your promise, let us show that we appreciate this free time.

2. *Aelred.* The fountain and source of friendship is love. There can be love without friendship, but friendship without love is impossible. Love proceeds either from nature, or from duty, from reason alone, or from affection alone, and sometimes from both simultaneously—from nature, as a mother loves her child; from duty, when through giving and receiving, some men are joined by special affection; from reason alone, as we love our enemies, not as the result of a spontaneous

91

inclination of the heart but from the necessity of precept; from affection alone, when anyone, because of bodily qualities only, such as beauty, strength, eloquence, inclines the affection of others to himself. 3. From reason and affection simultaneously, when he, whom reason urges should be loved because of the excellence of his virtue, steals into the soul of another by the mildness of his character and the charm of a praiseworthy life. In this way reason unites with affection so that the love is pure because of reason and sweet because of affection. Which of these types of love seems to you more advantageous to friendship?[1]

4. *Walter.* Indeed, the last, which contemplation of virtue forms and charm of character adorns. But I wish to know whether all whom we love in this manner should be admitted to that sweet mystery of friendship?

5. *Aelred.* In the first place, one ought to lay a solid foundation for spiritual love itself, and in this foundation its principles ought to be set down, so that those who are mounting straight up to its higher levels may not neglect or go beyond its foundation, but observe the greatest caution. That foundation is the love of God,[2] to which all things that either love or affection suggests, all that secretly any spirit or openly any friend recommends, must be referred. Moreover, one ought to observe carefully that whatever is built thereon conforms to the foundation. Have no doubt that whatever is seen as going beyond this foundation ought to be brought back into conformity with its plan and set right according to its nature.

6. And yet, not all whom we love should be received into friendship, for not all are found worthy of it. For since your

1. This passage finds a parallel in Spec car 3:20: "There is love proceeding from affection when the mind surrenders itself to feeling; love proceeding from reason, when the will unites itself to reason, and there may be a third kind of love compounded from these two when, for instance, reason, feeling, and will unite together. The first kind of love is delightful but dangerous, the second is dry but fruitful; the third kind possesses the advantages of them both, and alone is perfect. To the first love one is enticed by the experience of sweetness; to the second kind of love one is driven by cold reason; but in the third love, reason itself finds pleasure."

2. See below n. 54. Cf. also Amic 20; Spec car 1:33; 3:4, 19; Bernard of Clairvaux, *On Loving God,* 26, OB 3:140, CF 13; Ep 271, BLJ, Ep 341, pp. 419f.

friend is the companion of your soul, to whose spirit you join and attach yours, and so associate yourself that you wish to become one instead of two, since he is one to whom you entrust yourself as to another self, from whom you hide nothing, from whom you fear nothing,[3] you should, in the first place, surely choose one who is considered fitted for all this. Then he is to be tried, and so finally admitted. For friendship should be stable and manifest a certain likeness to eternity, persevering always in affection.[4] 7. And so we ought not, like children, change friends by reason of some vagrant whim.[5] For since there is no one more detestable than the man who injures friendship, and nothing torments the mind more than desertion or insult at the hands of a friend, a friend ought to be chosen with the utmost care and tested with extreme caution. But once admitted, he should be so borne with, so treated, so deferred to, that, as long as he does not withdraw irrevocably from the established foundation, he is yours, and you are his, in body as well as in psirit, so that there will be no division of minds, affections, wills, or judgments.[6] 8. You see, therefore, the four stages by which one climbs to the perfection of friendship: the first is selection, the second probation, the third admission, and the fourth perfect harmony in matters human and divine with charity and benevolence.[7]

9. *Walter.* I recall that you proved this definition satisfactorily in that first discussion of yours with your well loved Ivo; but since you treated of many types of friendship, I should like to know whether this definition includes them all.

10. *Aelred.* No; for since true friendship can exist only

---

3. *Duties* 133: "For what is a friend but a partner in love, to whom you unite and attach your soul and with whom you blend so as to desire from being two to become one, to whom you entrust yourself as to a second self, from whom you fear nothing, and from whom you demand nothing dishonorable for the sake of your own advantage."

4. Amic 67; *Duties* 127. Cf. also Cicero, *Timaeus,* 6.

5. *Duties* 127.

6. Cf. Conf. 16:24: "Charity cannot be made stable and undisturbed except among men of the same degree of virtue and of the same purpose."—SCh 54:243, CS 31.

7. Amic 20.

among the good[8] who can exhibit neither wish nor action detrimental to faith or good morals, this definition naturally does not embrace every friendship but only that friendship which is true.

11. *Gratian.* Why should not that definition which pleased me so much before yesterday's discussion be equally approved, namely, the one which defines friendship as a community of likes and dislikes?[9]

12. *Aelred.* Certainly. Among those whose habits have been corrected, whose life is well-ordered and whose affections are controlled, I think your definition need not be rejected.

13. *Walter.* Let Gratian see to it that these conditions be found not only in himself but also in the one he loves so that he will have the same likes and dislikes as his friend. Wishing nothing for himself, let him neither grant anything that is unjust, dishonorable, or unbecoming. But we are waiting to learn from you more about those four stages which you mentioned above.

14. *Aelred.* First of all, then, let us deal with selection itself. Now there are certain vices such that, if anyone has been involved in them, he will not long preserve the laws or rights of friendship. Persons of this type should not readily be chosen for friendship; but if their life and habits be found pleasing in other respects, one should deal energetically with them, to the end that they may be healed and so considered fitted for friendship. Such persons are, for example, the irascible, the fickle, the suspicious, and the garrulous. 15. Indeed, it is difficult for one subject to the frenzy of anger not to rise up sometime against his friend, as it is written in Ecclesiasticus: "There is a friend that will disclose hatred and strife and reproaches."[10] Therefore Scripture says: "Be not a friend to an angry man, and do not walk with a furious man, lest he become a snare for your soul."[11] And Solomon: "Anger rests in the bosom of a fool."[12] And who does not think it impossible to preserve friendship for long with a fool?

8. Amic 65.
9. See above, Book I, note 35, p. 59.
10. Sir 6:9.
11. Prov 22:24f.
12. Eccles 7:10.

16. *Walter.* But we have seen you, if we are not mistaken, with deep devotion cultivate a friendship with a very irascible man, and we have heard, he was never hurt by you even to the end of his life, though he often offended you.

17. *Aelred.* There are some individuals who have a natural bent toward anger, yet who are accustomed so to restrain and overcome this passion that they never give way to those five vices which Scripture testifies dissolve and break friendship.[13] However they may occasionally offend a friend by a thoughtless word or act or by a zeal that fails in discretion. If it happens that we have received such men into our friendship, we must bear with them patiently. And since their affection toward us is established with certainly, if then there is any excess in word or action, this ought to be put up with as being in a friend, or at least our admonition of his fault ought to be administered painlessly and even pleasantly.

18. *Gratian.* A few days ago that friend of yours, whom many think you prefer to all of us, was, so we thought, overcome by anger, and said and did something that everyone could see displeased you. Yet we do not believe or see that he has in any degree lost favor with you. Hence we are not a little surprised that, when we speak together, you will not neglect anything that pleases him no matter how trivial it may be, yet he cannot bear even trifles for your sake.

19. *Walter.* Gratian is far bolder than I am; for I was aware of these facts, but knowing your feeling toward him, I did not dare to say anything to you about the matter.

20. *Aelred.* Certainly that man is very dear to me. Having once received him into my friendship, I can never do otherwise than love him. Therefore, if perhaps I was stronger than he was in this instance, and since the wills of both did not fuse into one, it was easier for me to yield my will than he his. And since there was no question of any dishonor being involved, and as confidence was not violated, or virtue lessened, it was right for me to yield to my friend that I might bear with him when he seemed to have transgressed, and that, when his peace was endangered, I might prefer his will to mine.

21. *Walter.* But since your former friend has passed away,

13. Sir 22:27. See below, n. 56, p. 108.

and this other has satisfied you, although we do not see how, I would like to have you explain to us those five vices by which friendship is so injured as to be dissolved, in order that we may be able to avoid those who ought in no wise be chosen as friends.

22. *Aelred.* Listen, then, not to my words, but to Scripture: "He that upbraids his friend, breaks friendship. Although he has drawn a sword at a friend, despair not; for there may be a returning to a friend. If he opens a sad mouth, fear not."[14] Consider what this means. If your friend, overcome by anger, chances to draw a sword or utter a grievous word, if, as though not loving you, he for a time withdraws himself from you, if sometimes he prefers his own counsel to yours, if he disagrees with you in any opinion or discussion, do not think your friendship must be dissolved because of these differences. 23. "For," says Scripture, "there may be a reconciliation with your friend except in the case of upbraiding, reproach, pride, disclosing of secrets or a treacherous wound; for in all these cases a friend will flee away."[15]

Let us then more carefully consider these five vices, that we may not bind ourselves by the ties of friendship to persons whom either the fury of anger or some other passion is wont to incite to these vices. Slander, indeed, injures reputation and extinguishes love. For such is the wickedness of men, that whenever a friend makes a charge against a friend under the impulse of anger, even though it is not believed, it is yet broadcast as if it were the utterance of a confidant of secrets. 24. For just as many are delighted at praise of themselves, so too do they find joy in reproaches against their neighbors. What is more impious than reproach which suffuses the countenance of an innocent man with a pitiable blush even when the charge is false? But what is less to be endured than pride, which excludes the remedy of humility and admission of guilt by which alone the broken friendship could have been healed?

14. Sir 22:26f.
15. Sir 22:27. It would be well to note here that Aelred is following the Vulgate which has two distinct words which are translated here as: "upbraiding and reproach"; whereas the Greek text, which the Revised Standard Version (22:22) follows, has only one term.

It renders a man bold in wrongdoing and passionate in recrimination. Then follows the revelation of hidden things, that is, of secrets, than which nothing is more base, nothing more detestable, leaving no love and no charm between friends, but filling all with the bitterness of indignation and sprinkling all with the venom of hatred and grief. 25. Hence it is written: "He that discloses the secret of a friend loses his credit."[16] And a little later: "To disclose the secrets of a friend leaves no hope to an unhappy soul."[17] For what is more unfortunate than the man who loses faith and languishes in despair. The last vice by which friendship is dissolved is treacherous persecution, which is nothing other than secret detraction. A treacherous blow indeed, it is the death-dealing blow of the serpent and the asp. "If a serpent bite in silence," says Solomon, "he is no better who backbites secretly."[18] 26. Therefore, should you discover anyone habituated to these vices, you ought to avoid him, nor, until he repents, should he be chosen for friendship. Let us renounce slander, the avenger of which is God. Shimei, attacking holy David with insults as he was fleeing from the face of Absalom, was, according to the testamentary words which the dying father bequeathed to his son, decreed by the authority of the Holy Spirit to be worthy of death.[19] Let us then shun recriminations. The unhappy Nabel of Carmel, reproaching David with his servitude and his flight, merited to be cut down by the Lord and killed.[20] But if we chance to have failed in the law of friendship toward anyone, let us shun pride and seek to win back the favor of our friend by some humble service. 27. When King David mercifully offered friendship to Hanun, the son of Nabash, a friendship such as he had formerly displayed to Nabash, the king of the children of Ammon, Hanun, arrogant and ungrateful to his friend, added contumely to contempt.[21] For this reason fire and sword together consumed him as well as his people and

16. Sir 27:17.
17. Sir 27:24.
18. Eccles 10:11.
19. 2 Sam 16:3ff; 1 Kings 2:8f.
20. 1 Sam 25:10, 38.
21. 1 Chron 19:1ff.; 2 Sam 10:1ff; 12:26ff.

his cities. But above all things, let us consider it a sacrilege to reveal the secrets of friends, an act by which confidence is lost and despair is borne in upon the captive soul. Hence it is that the impious Ahithophel, casting his lot with the parricide Absalom, after he had betrayed to him David's plan, presently saw that the plan he himself had proposed in opposition was not being put into effect; thereupon he took his own life by hanging—an end worthy of a traitor.[22] 28. Finally, let us consider it the poison of friendship to slander a friend, an act which caused the face of Mary to be covered with leprosy, and caused her to be cast outside the camp for six days, and to be deprived of association with the people.[23]

Not only men of excessive anger but also the fickle and the suspicious should be avoided in this selection of friends.[24] For since a great fruit of friendship is the security whereby you entrust and commit yourself to a friend, how can there be any security in the love of him who is tossed about by every wind, who consents to every counsel? The disposition of such a man, like soft clay, receives and fashions diverse and opposing images the livelong day, at the whim of him who wishes to impress them. 29. Besides, what is more in accord with friendship than a certain mutual peace and tranquility of heart, which the suspicious man never knows, since he is never at rest?[25] In truth the suspicious man is ever ridden by his curiosity, which pricks him with relentless spurs and has an inexhaustible supply of fuel for the fires of uneasiness and anxiety that burn under him. For if he sees his friend speaking secretly with anyone, he thinks he is betrayed. If his friend shows himself kind to another, or pleasant, he cries out that he himself is loved the less. If his friend rebukes him, he interprets this as hatred. If his friend believes him worthy of praise, he charges falsely that he is being mocked. 30. Neither do I think the one who is garrulous should be chosen, because a talkative man will not be justified.[26] "Do you see,"

22. 2 Sam 15:12ff.; 17:1ff.
23. Num 12:1ff.
24. Amic 62.
25. RB 64:16.
26. Ps 139:2; Job 11:2.

says the Wise Man, "a person over-ready with his tongue? There is more hope for a fool than for such a one."²⁷ That man, therefore, should be chosen as your friend whom the fury of anger does not disturb, nor instability divide, nor suspicion consume, nor garrulity sunder from the gravity which ought to be his. It is particularly advantageous for you to choose one who conforms to your habits, who harmonizes with your disposition. "Indeed, among dissimilar characters," as blessed Ambrose remarks, "friendship cannot exist; therefore, the grace of each ought to be mutually consonant."²⁸

31. *Walter.* But where can such a man be found, one who is neither irascible, nor unstable, nor suspicious? For as to the over-talkative man, he cannot escape notice.

32. *Aelred.* Although it is not easy to find one who is never moved by these passions, there surely are many who are found to be superior to all of them; men who suppress anger with patience, restrain levity by preserving gravity, drive out suspicions by the contemplation of love. I should say that such men ought to be chosen by preference for friendship on the ground that they are better trained in it. Because they conquer vice with virtue, their friendship is the more enduring as their resistance to temptation is the more valiant.

33. *Gratian.* Please, do not be angry if I speak. With respect to that friend of yours, of whom we made mention a little while ago, and whom, we do not doubt, you have received into your friendship, I should like to know whether he seems irascible to you.

34. *Aelred.* He is, indeed; but in friendship, hardly at all.

35. *Gratian.* What do you mean, not to be angry in friendship?

36. *Aelred.* You do not doubt that friendship exists between us?

Gratian. Not at all.

Aelred. when have you heard of anger, strife, dissensions, rivalries, or disputes arising between us?

Gratian. Never, but we attribute this not to his, but to your patience.

27. Prov 29:20 (Septuagint).
28. *Duties* 132. Cf. Amic 50.

37. *Aelred.* You are mistaken. For anger which is not held in check by affection can in no wise be checked by the patience of some other person. On the contrary, patience excites the irascible man to fury[29] and he hopes to get a crumb of comfort from the possibility that another may show himself to be his match in vituperation. Indeed, he about whom we are now speaking, preserves the law of friendship toward me in such a way that I can restrain an outburst at any time by a mere nod, even when it is already breaking forth into speech, so that he never reveals in public what is displeasing but always waits till we are alone to unburden his mind's thought. 38. Now, if, instead of friendship, nature prescribed this course of action to him, I would judge him neither so virtuous nor so worthy of praise. If, indeed, as is sometimes the case, my feeling differs from his, we give in to each other so that sometimes he yields to me, but generally I yield to him.

39. *Walter.* Gratian has had sufficient attention. Now I should like to have you explain this to me: suppose one should somewhat heedlessly chance to contact friendship with characters such as those whom you said a little while ago we should avoid, or suppose those who you said should be chosen should fall into these vices or perhaps even into worse ones, what sort of loyalty ought then to be preserved toward them and what sort of favor ought to be shown them?

40. *Aelred.* Obviously these things should, if possible, be guarded against in the act of choosing friends and also during their probation, so that, indeed, we may not form intimacies too quickly, particularly with those unworthy of such regard. Now, they are worthy of friendship in whose very selves there is reason why they should be loved.[30] And yet, even in those who are thought to have been tried and found worthy, faults often betray themselves, at one time to the injury of their friends, at another to that of strangers; and in the latter case,

---

29. Cf. Conf. 16:18: "There is another abuse committed by some who think they are patient. . . . We do not reply to our brethren when they provoke us. This grave and affected silence . . . irritates them infinitely more than the most sarcastic speech or injurious words."—SCh 54:237-239, CS 31. Also, Seneca, *De ira,* 3:8; tr. A. Stewart, "Of Anger," *Minor Dialogues* (London: Ball, 1889), p. 83.

30. Amic 79.

the disgrace of their action falls back upon their friends.[31] With such friends all care must be taken that they may be made to amend their lives. 41. But if this is impossible, I think friendship should not be broken off or dissolved, but, as someone has well said, "it should rather be unstitched little by little,[32] unless perchance some insufferable offense flames out to full view, so that it is neither right nor honorable not to effect an immediate estrangement or separation."[33] For if a friend undertakes anything either against his father or against his country which demands sudden and hurried correction, the demands of friendship will not be violated, if he is proclaimed a public and private enemy. 42. There are other faults for which, we think, friendship should not be broken off, as we have said, but dissolved gradually, yet in such a way that they do not result in enmities, from which spring quarrels, imprecations, and slanders.[34] For it is most shameful to wage a war of this kind with a man with whom you have lived on terms of intimacy.[35] 43. For even if in all these ways you are assailed by him whom you had taken into your friendship (for with some men it is the way that, when they have so lived that they no longer deserve to be loved, if by chance some misfortune befalls them, they put the blame on their friend. They say that he has sinned against the laws of friendship, and every counsel which their friend gave they hold suspect. When they are unmasked and their fault is made public, not having anything else to do, they heap hatred and insults upon their friend, slandering him in corners, whispering in the dark, and telling lies to excuse themselves and accuse others[36]); 44. if, therefore, I say, you are attacked in all such ways after friendship has been severed, as long as the abuses are tolerable, they ought to be endured. This honor should be accorded to old friendship, that the fault should be in him who commits, but not to him who suffers, the wrong.[37] Friendship, indeed, is eternal;

31. Amic 76.
32. Cato as quoted in Amic 76. Cf. Cicero, *De officiis*, 1:120; Seneca, *Epist. ad Lucil.*, 22; Jerome, Ep 8 (PL 22:342).
33. Amic 76.
34. Amic 78.
35. Amic 77.
36. Iesu 21; CF 2:28-29; Ohner 8, PL 195:3890, CF 26.
37. Amic 78.

hence: "He that is a friend loves at all times."[38] If the one whom you love offends you, continue to love him despite the hurt. His conduct may compel the withdrawal of friendship, but never of love. Be concerned as much as you can for his welfare, safeguard his reputation, and never betray the secrets of his friendship, even though he should betray yours.

45. *Walter.* What are these faults, pray, for which you say friendship should be dissolved little by little?

46. *Aelred.* Those five which we described a little while ago, but especially the revelation of secrets and the hidden stings of detraction. To these five we add a sixth, namely, if your friend has injured those whom you are bound to love equally well, and if, even after he has been called to task, he continued to be an occasion of ruin and scandal to those for whose well-being you are responsible, especially when the infamy of these crimes is damaging to your own good name. For love ought not to outweigh religion, or faith, or charity toward one's neighbor, or the welfare of the people. 47. King Ahsuerus suspended on a cross the most haughty Aman, whom he had cherished above all others as his friend, preferring the welfare of his people and the love of his wife to the friendship which Aman had wounded by deceitful counsels.[39] And Jael, the wife of Heber the Klenite, although there was peace between Sisera and the house of Heber, nevertheless, preferring the welfare of her people to this friendship, put Sisera himself to sleep with a nail and hammer.[40] The holy prophet David according to the law of friendship ought to have spared the relations of Jonathan. Nevertheless, hearing from the Lord that the people had suffered continually from hunger during three years "on account of Saul and his bloody house because he had killed the Gibeonites," he gave seven of Saul's relations to the Gibeonites to be punished.[41] 48. But I would not have you overlook this point, that between perfect friends, between friends who have been wisely chosen and prudently tested and

38. Prov 17:17.
39. Esther 7.
40. Judg 4:17ff.
41. 2 Sam 21:1ff.

are united by a genuinely spiritual friendship, no disagree-
ments can possibly arise. For when friendship has made of two
one, just as that which is one cannot be divided, so also friendship cannot be separated from itself. Therefore it is evident
that a friendship, which permits of division, was never, in the
respect in which it is injured, a true friendship at all, because
"friendship which can end, was never true friendship."[42] 49.
On the other hand, a friendship is the more laudable, and
gives the greater proof of being a virtue, in proportion as the
friend who has been wronged preserves it undiminished, loving
him by whom he is no longer loved, honoring him by whom he
is scorned, blessing him by whom he is cursed, and doing good
to him who plots evil against him.

50. *Walter.* Now, therefore, can friendship be said to be dissolved, if such dispositions are to be manifested to the former
friend by him who "dissolves" friendship?

51. *Aelred.* Four elements in particular seem to pertain to
friendship: namely, love and affection, security and happiness.
Love implies the rendering of services with benevolence, affection, an inward pleasure that manifests itself exteriorly;
security, a revelation of all counsels and confidences without
fear and suspicion; happiness, a pleasing and friendly sharing
of all events which occur, whether joyful or sad, of all thoughts,
whether harmful or useful, of everything taught or learned.[43]
52. Do you see in what respects friendship should be withdrawn from those who deserve to lose it? Surely that interior
delight is withdrawn which drank continually from the heart
of the friend; security is lost, by which it revealed its secrets
to a friend; happiness is put aside, which friendly conversation
produced. Therefore, that familiarity, in which such things
find their place, must be denied a former friend, but love
should not be withdrawn; yet all this should be done with a
certain moderation and reverence, so that, if there has not
been too great a shock, some traces of the former friendship
always seem to remain.

53. *Gratian.* I certainly agree with what you say.

42. Jerome, Ep 3:6, PL 22:335.
43. Spec car 3:40.

Aelred. Now turn your attention to selection, if I have said enough on these present points.

Walter. I should like a summary of the matter discussed to be given us in a brief recapitulation.

54. *Aelred.* I shall do as you wish. We have said that love is the source of friendship, not love of any sort whatever, but that which proceeds from reason and affection simultaneously, which, indeed, is pure because of reason and sweet because of affection. Then we said that a foundation of friendship should be laid in the love of God, to which all things which are proposed should be referred, and these ought to be examined as to whether they conform to the foundation or are at variance with it. 55. Then we thought that one should pay attention to the four steps which lead up to the heights of perfect friendship; for a friend ought first to be selected, next tested, then finally admitted, and from then on treated as a friend deserves. And speaking of selection, we excluded the quarrelsome, the irascible, the fickle, the suspicious, and the loquacious; and yet not all, but only those who are unable or unwilling to regulate or restrain these passions. For many are affected by these disturbances in such a manner that their perfection is not only in no way injured, but their virtue is even more laudably increased by the restraint of these passions. 56. For men, who, as though unbridled, are carried away headlong under the impulse of these passions, inevitably slip and fall into those vices by which friendship, as Scripture testifies, is wounded and dissolved; namely, insults, reproaches, betrayal of secrets, pride, and the stroke of treachery.[44] 57. If, nevertheless, you suffer all these evils from him whom you once received into friendship, we said that your friendship should not be broken off immediately, but dissolved little by little, and that such reverence should be maintained for the former friendship, that, although you withdraw your confidence from him, yet you never withdraw your love, refuse your aid, or deny him your advice. But if his frenzy breaks out even to blasphemies and calumny, do you, nevertheless, yield to the bonds of friendship, yield to charity, so that the blame will reside with

44. Sir 22:27. See above, note 15.

him who inflicts, not with him who bears, the injury. 58. Furthermore, if he is found to be a peril to his father, to his country, to his fellow-citizens, to his dependents or to his friends, the bond of familiarity ought to be broken immediately; love for one man should not take precedence over the ruin of many. To prevent such misfortunes one should be cautious in choosing a friend, that one be chosen whom fury does not goad on to such evils, nor levity induce, nor loquacity drive headlong; nor suspicion carry off; especially should one be chosen who does not differ too much from your character, and is not of harmony with your temperament. 59. But since we are speaking of true friendship, which cannot exist except among the good, we make no mention of those concerning whom there can be no doubt that they ought not to be chosen, namely, those who are base, avaricious, ambitious, slanderous. Now, then, if we have discussed selection sufficiently for you, let us then pass on to probation.

Walter. This is truly opportune, for I have my eye glued on the door for fear that someone may break in who will either put an end to our delights, or mingle some bitterness therewith, or introduce something trivial.

60. *Gratian.* The cellarer is coming; if you grant him admittance, you will have no opportunity of proceeding further, But see, I am guarding the door; do, Father, go on as you have begun.

61. *Aelred.* There are four qualities which must be tested in a friend: loyalty, right intention, discretion, and patience, that you may entrust yourself to him securely. The right intention, that he may expect nothing from your friendship except God and its natural good. Discretion, that he may understand what is to be done in behalf of a friend, what is to be sought from a friend, what sufferings are to be endured for his sake, upon what good deeds he is to be congratulated; and, since we think that a friend should sometimes be corrected, he must know for what faults this should be done, as well as the manner, the time, and the place. Finally, patience, that he may not grieve when rebuked, or despise or hate the one inflicting the rebuke, and that he may not be unwilling to bear every adversity for the sake of his friend.

62. There is nothing more praiseworthy in friendship than loyalty, which seems to be its nurse and guardian. It proves itself a true companion in all things—adverse and prosperous, joyful and sad, pleasing and bitter—beholding with the same eye the humble and the lofty, the poor and the rich, the strong and the weak, the healthy and the infirm. A truly loyal friend sees nothing in his friend but his heart. Embracing virtue in its proper place, and putting aside all else as if it were outside him, the faithful friend does not value them much if they are present, and does not seek them if they are absent. 63. Moreover, loyalty is hidden in prosperity, but conspicuous in adversity. A friend is tested in necessity.[45] The rich man's friends abound,[46] but whether they are true friends, intervening adversity proves. Solomon says: "He that is a friend loves at all times, and a brother is proved in distress."[47] And rebuking infidelity he says: "To trust an unfaithful man in the time of trouble is like a rotten tooth and weary foot."[48]

64. *Gratian.* But if no adversity ever spoils our prosperity, how will the loyalty of a friend be proved?

65. *Aelred.* There are many other ways in which the fidelity of a friend is proved, though ill-fortune is the best. For, as we have said before, there is nothing which wounds friendship more than the betrayal of one's secret counsels. Indeed, the Gospel sentence reads: "He that is faithful in that which is little, will be faithful in that which is great."[49] Therefore, to those friends, for whom thus far we have thought probation necessary, we ought not confide to them all our profound secrets, but at first, external or little things about which one does not care a great deal whether they be concealed or exposed; yet this should be done with very great caution as if these smaller matters should do harm if betrayed, but would be of service if concealed. 66. If your friend has been found faithful in these smaller matters, do not hesitate to test him in greater. But if rumor chance to spread anything harmful about you, if anyone through malice has injured your reputa-

45. *Duties* 129, p. 88; Cf. Bernard of Clairvaux, Ep 125:1, BLJ 128, p. 190.
46. Prov 14:20.
47. Prov 17:17.
48. Prov 25:19.
49. Lk 16:10. Aelred actually does not give the text verbatim but changes *in minimo* to *in modico* and *in majori* to *in multo*.

tion, and your friend believes nothing of these tales, is moved by no suspicion, and is disturbed by no doubt, you should have no further hesitation concerning his loyalty, but be very happy at having a friend who is safe and stable.

67. *Gratian.* Just now I call to mind that friend of yours across the sea,[50] whom you have often mentioned to us, the one whom you proved the truest and most faithful friend by a test of this kind. When certain individuals bore false witness against you, he not only did not relinquish his faith in you, but was not moved by any hesitation whatsoever; something you did not think you could presume upon even from your dearest friend, the old sacristan of Clairvaux.[51] But since we have said enough on the test of loyalty, proceed to explain the remaining points.

68. *Aelred.* We have said that the intention, too, should be proved. This is especially necessary, for there are very many who recognize nothing as good in human affairs, except what bears fruit in time. Such men love their friends as they do their cattle, from which they hope to derive some good.[52] They, indeed, lack genuine and spiritual friendship, which ought to be sought on account of God and for its own sake, they do not reflect upon the natural exemplar of love where the power of friendship may easily be detected both as to its quality and its greatness.[53] 69. Our Lord and Savior himself has written for us the formula of true friendship when he said: You shall love your neighbor as yourself."[54] Behold the mirror. You love yourself. Yes, especially if you love God, if you are such a person as we have described as worthy of being chosen for friendship. But tell me, do you think you should expect any reward from yourself for this love of yours? No, indeed, not the least, for from the very nature of things each one is dear to himself. Unless, therefore, you transfer his same affection to the other, loving him gratuitously, in that from the very nature of things in himself your friend seems dear, you can-

---

50. Dubois identifies this friend with the one Aelred speaks of below, n. 124— *L'amitié*, p. 139, n. 1.

51. Dubois identifies this sacristan of Clairvaux as Blessed Gerard, the brother of St Bernard—*ibid*.

52. Amic 79.

53. Amic 80.

54. Mt 22:39.

not savor what true friendship is. 70. For then truly he whom you love will be another self, if you have transformed your love of self to him.[55] "For friendship is not tribute," as St Ambrose says, "but a thing full of beauty, full of grace. It is a virtue, not a trade, because it is bought with love, not money, because it is acquired by competition in generosity, not by a haggling over its prices."[56] Therefore the intention of the one whom you have chosen must subtly be tested, that he may not wish to be joined in friendship to you according to the hope of some advantage, thinking friendship mercenary and not gratuitous.

Moreover, friendships among the poor are generally more secure than those among the rich,[57] since poverty takes away the hope of gain in such a way as not to decrease the love of friendship but rather to increase it. 71. And so towards the wealthy one acts flatteringly, but towards the poor no one pretends to be other than he is. Whatever is given to a poor man is a true gift, for the friendship of the poor is devoid of envy. We have made these statements that we may prove the character of our friends, not that we may appraise their financial rating. In this way, then, is intention proved. Should you see that your friend is more desirous of your goods than of yourself, always lying in wait for something which can be gained for himself through your effort: honor, glory, riches, freedom. If, in these matters, some worthier person is preferred to him, and especially if the object of his quest is not in your power, under these circumstances you will easily perceive with what intention he clings to you.

72. And now let us examine the quality of discretion. There are some men who are so perverse, not to say shameless,[58] as to wish a friend to be in character what they themselves cannot be. These are they who also bear impatiently the petty faults of their friends and rebuke them severely; and who, lacking discretion, neglect important matters but are aroused at all minute points. They confuse everything with-

55. *Ibid.* Cf. Seneca, *De Moribus,* 20; Bernard of Clairvaux, Ep 53, BLJ 56, p. 84.
56. *Duties* 3:133, p. 89.
57. *Duties* 134, *ibid.*
58. Amic 82.

out regarding the fitting place, the due season, not the person
to whom one may fittingly reveal something, or from whom
such matters must be concealed. For this reason, the discretion of him whom you choose should be proved, lest,
if you associate with yourself in friendship anyone thoughtless or imprudent, you gain for yourself daily controversies
and quarrels. 73. Indeed, it is easy enough to see that this virtue
is necessary in friendship, since, if anyone lacks it, he is like
a ship bereft of its pilot, borne along by every shifting and
irrational movement. Many situations cannot fail to be at
hand for a trying of the patience of him whom you desire as
a friend, for you must needs rebuke him whom you love,
and sometimes it is well, as it were, purposely to do this more
severely, in order that the patience of your friend may be
tested or tried.[59] 74. This certainly must be noted, that, although such faults as offend the soul be found in him whom
you are proving, be they in the thoughtless revelation of some
confidence, or the desire of some temporal gain, or a somewhat indiscreet rebuke, or overpassing the bounds of due
gentleness, do not withdraw immediately from your proposed
love or choice, as long as any hope of correction appears.
And let no one in choosing or testing friends weary of being
solicitous, since the fruit of this labor is the medicine of life
and the most solid foundation of immortality.[60] 75. For since
many men are experts in multiplying treasures and in feeding,
choosing and comparing oxen and asses, and sheep and goats,
and certain signs for recognition in all these matters are not
lacking, it is madness not to give the same unwearied attention
to acquiring and testing friends, and to learning certain marks
whereby those whom we have chosen as friends may be proved
suitable for friendship.[61] But surely a certain impulse of love
should be guarded against, which runs ahead of judgment and
takes away the power of testing. 76. Accordingly it is the part
of the prudent man to pause, to hold in check this impulse,[62]
to moderate his good will, and to proceed gradually in affection

59. Amic 88.
60. Sir 6:16.
61. Amic 62. The same idea is found in Xenophon, *Memorables,* 2:4.
62. Amic 63.

until he may give himself up wholly and commit himself to his now proven friend.

Walter. I confess that I am still moved by the opinion of those men who think they live more safely without friends of this type.

Aelred. This is astonishing, since without friends absolutely no life can be happy.[63]

Walter. Why, I ask you?

77. *Aelred.* Let us imagine that the whole human race has been taken out of the world leaving you as the sole survivor. Now behold before you all the delights and riches of the world, —gold, silver, precious stones, walled cities, turreted camps, spacious buildings, sculptures, and paintings.[64] And consider yourself also as transformed to that ancient state, having all creatures under your dominion, "all sheep and oxen; moreover, the beasts of the fields, the birds of the air, and the fishes of the sea that pass through the paths of the sea."[65] Tell me, now, whether without a companion you could enjoy all these possessions?

Water. No, not at all.

78. *Aelred.* But suppose there were one person, whose language you did not know, of whose customs you were ignorant, whose love and heart lay concealed from you?

Walter. If I could not by some signs make him a friend, I should prefer to have no one at all rather than to have such a one.

Aelred. If, however, one were at hand whom you loved as much as yourself and by whom you were similarly loved, would not all these possessions, which before seemed bitter, become sweet and full of savor?

---

63. Cf. Cicero, *Pro Plancio*, 80; tr. N. H. Watts, *Cicero, The Speeches,* Loeb Classical Series (Cambridge: Harvard, 1935) p. 513.

64. Amic 87: "This especially would be granted if it could happen that God should remove us from the companionship of men and place us somewhere in solitude, and there provide us with an abundance of those things that nature craves for, taking away, at the same time, all hope of seeing a fellow creature. Who would have such a heart of steel as not to find such existence intolerable? Who would not lose enjoyment in all other pleasures in such solitude? "

65. Ps 8:8f.

Walter. Indeed, they would.

Aelred. Would you not think yourself happier in proportion to the number of such companions?

Walter. By all means.

79. *Aelred.* This is that extraordinary and great happiness which we await, with God himself acting and diffusing, between himself and his creatures whom he has uplifted, among the very degrees and orders which he has distinguished, among the individual souls whom he has chosen, so much friendship and charity, that thus each loves another as he does himself; and that, by this means, just as each one rejoices in his own, so does he rejoice in the good fortune of another, and thus the happiness of each one individually is the happiness of all, and the universality of all happiness is the possession of each individual. 80. There one finds no hiding of thoughts, no dissembling of affection. This is true and eternal friendship, which begins in this life and is perfected in the next, which here belongs to the few where few are good, but there belongs to all where all are good. Here, probation is necessary since there is a mingling of wise and unwise; there they need no probation, since an angelic and, in a certain manner, divine perfection beatifies them. To this pattern, then, let us compare our friends, whom we are to love as we do ourselves, whose confidences are to be laid bare to us, to whom our confidences are likewise to be disclosed, who are to be firm and stable and constant in all things. Do you think there is any human being who does not wish to be loved? [66]

Walter. I think not.

81. *Aelred.* If you were to see a man living among many people, suspecting all and fearing all as plotters against his own life, cherishing no one and thinking himself cherished by none, would you not judge such a man most wretched?[67]

Walter. Yes, very evidently so.

Aelred. Therefore you will not deny that he is most fortunate who rests in the inmost hearts of those among whom he lives,

66. Amic 62.
67. Amic 52.

loving all and being loved by all,[68] whom neither suspicion severs nor fear cuts off from this sweetest tranquility.[69]

Walter. Excellently said, and most truly.

82. *Aelred.* But, perhaps, it is difficult to find this perfection with respect to all in this present life, since that is reserved for us in the life to come, yet shall we not consider ourselves happier in proportion as more individuals of this type abound for us?

The day before yesterday, as I was walking the round of the cloister of the monastery, the brethren were sitting around forming as it were a most loving crown. In the midst, as it were, of the delights of paradise with the leaves, flowers, and fruits of each single tree, I marveled. In that multitude of brethren I found no one whom I did not love, and no one by whom, I felt sure, I was not loved. I was filled with such joy that it surpassed all the delights of this world. I felt, indeed, my spirit transfused into all and the affection of all to have passed into me, so that I could say with the Prophet: "Behold, how good and how pleasant it is for brethren to dwell together in unity."[70]

Gratian. Are we not to think that you have taken into your friendship all those whom you thus love and by whom you are so loved?

83. *Aelred.* We embrace very many with every affection, but yet in such a way that we do not admit them to the secrets of friendship, which consists especially in the revelation of all our confidences and plans. Whence it is that the Lord in the Gospel says: "I will not now call you servants but friends";[71] and then adding the reason for which they are considered worthy of the name of friend: "because all things, whatsoever I have heard of my Father, I have made known to you."[72] And in another place: "You are my friends, if you do the things that I command you."[73] From these words, as Saint

68. Cf. Spec car 1:34; *De Bello Standardii* (PL 195:708).
69. Spec car 1:34. See above, n. 29.
70. Ps 132:1.
71. Jn 15:15.
72. *Ibid.*
73. Jn 15:14.

Ambrose says, "He gives the formula of friendship for us to follow: namely, that we do the will of our friend, that we disclose to our friend whatever confidences we have in our hearts, and that we be not ignorant of his confidences. Let us lay bare to him our heart and let him disclose his to us. For a friend hides nothing. If he is true, he pours forth his soul just as the Lord Jesus poured forth the mysteries of the Father."[74] 84. Thus speaks Ambrose. How many, therefore, do we love before whom it would be imprudent to lay bare our souls and pour out our inner hearts! men whose age or feeling or discretion is not sufficient to bear such revelations.

85. *Walter.* This friendship is so sublime and perfect that I dare not aspire to it. For me and our friend Gratian that type of friendship suffices which your Augustine describes: namely, to converse and jest together, with good-will to humor one another, to read together, to discuss matters together, together to trifle, and together to be in earnest; to differ at times without ill-humor, as a man would do with himself, and even by a very infrequent disagreement to give zest to our very numerous agreements; to teach one another something, or to learn from one another; with impatience to long for one another when absent, and with joy to receive one another when returning. 86. By these and similar indications emanating from the hearts of those who love and are loved in turn, through the countenance, the tongue, the eyes, and a thousand pleasing movements, to fuse our spirits by tinder, as it were, and out of many to make but one. This is what we think we should love in our friends, so that our conscience will be its own accuser, if we have not loved him who in turn loves us, or if we have not returned love to him who first loved us.[75]

87. *Aelred.* This type of friendship belongs to the carnal, and especially to the young people, such as they once were, Augustine and the friend of whom he was then speaking. And yet this friendship except for trifles and deceptions, if nothing dishonorable enters into it, is to be tolerated in the hope of more abundant grace, as the beginnings, so to say, of a holier

74. *Duties* 135, p. 89.
75. *Duties* 4:8f, pp. 48f.

friendship.[76] By these beginnings, with a growth in piety and in constant zeal for things of the spirit, with the growing seriousness of maturer years and the illumination of the spiritual senses,[77] they may, with purer affections, mount to loftier heights from, as it were, a region close by, just as yesterday we said that the friendship of man could be easily translated into a friendship for God himself because of the similarity existing between both.

88. But now it is time that we examine the points, one after another, as to how friendship is to be cultivated. Loyalty, then, is the foundation of stability and constancy in friendship, for nothing is stable that is unfaithful.[78] Indeed, the frank, the congenial, and the sympathetic, and those who can be stirred by like qualities, ought to be friends to one another; and all of these qualities pertain to fidelity.[79] For a changeable and crafty character cannot be faithful, nor can those who have not like interests and mutual agreements on like matters be stable or faithful in friendship. 89. Above all things, however, suspicion ought to be avoided, for it is the poison of friendship. Let us never think evil regarding a friend, or believe or agree with anyone speaking evil of our friend. And here let us add affability in speech, cheerfulness of countenance, suavity in manners, serenity in the expression of the eyes, matters in which there is to be found no slight relish to friendship.[80] For sadness and a rather severe demeanor give one a certain appearance of gravity, but friendship ought to be, so to say, rather relaxed at times; it ought to be somewhat free and mild, and rather incline to congeniality and easiness of approach without levity and dissipation.[81] 90. It is also

76. Amic 22.

77. The theme of "illumination" is a common one among the Cistercians who undoubtedly draw upon St Augustine for this. For a study of this theme, see J. Morson and H. Costello, Introduction, in *The Liturgical Sermons of Guerric of Igny*, vol. 1, CF 8:xxxviii-xlvi.

78. Amic 65.

79. Cf. *ibid.*

80. Cf. Spec car 1:34; *Third Sermon for the Feast of the Epiphany* (CF 23); *Second Sermon for the Feast of the Annunciation (ibid.)*; Cassidorus, *De anima*, 13, ed. J. W. Halporn in *Traditio* 16 (1960) p. 39.

81. Amic 66.

a law of friendship that a superior must be on a plane of equality with the inferior.[82] For often, indeed, persons of inferior rank or order of dignity or knowledge are assumed into friendship by persons of greater excellence. In this case it behooves them to despise and esteem as nothing and as vanity what is but an addition to nature, and always to direct their attention to the beauty of friendship, which is not adorned with silken garments or gems, is not expanded by possessions, does not grow fat with delicacies, does not abound in riches, is not exalted by honors, is not puffed up by dignities. Coming back to the principle of friendship's origin, let them consider with care the quality which nature has given, rather than the external trappings which avarice affords to human kind. 91. Therefore in friendship, which is the perfect gift of nature and grace alike, let the lofty descend, the lowly ascend; the rich be in want, the poor become rich; and thus let each communicate his condition to the other, so that equality may be the result. Hence it is written: "He that had much, had nothing over; and he that had little, had no want."[83] Never, therefore, prefer yourself to your friend; but if you chance to find yourself the superior in those things which we have mentioned, then do not hesitate to abase yourself before your friend, to give him your confidence, to praise him if he is shy, and to confer honor upon him in inverse proportion to that warranted by his lowliness and poverty.[84] 92. Jonathan, that excellent youth, paying no heed to a royal crown or to the hope of regal power, entered upon a covenant with David.[85] He made the servant, David, an equal in friendship in the Lord. He preferred him to himself, when David was driven into flight before Saul, when he was hiding in the desert, when he

82. Amic 69. Jerome, *Commentary on Matthew*, 2:7 (PL 25:1219). Cf. Augustine, *De Genesi ad litteram imperfectus liber*, 18 (PL 34:243); also Jerome on Micah, c. 8: "Friendship either finds equals or makes them. Where there is inequality, one takes pre-eminence, and the other bears subjection. But this is not so much friendship as adulation. Hence we read somewhere: 'Let your friend be as your own soul.' And the poet, praying for his friend, says, 'preserve the half of my soul.' " (PL 25:1218f.).

83. 2 Cor 8:15. Cf. Ex 16:18.

84. Amic 72. Cf. *Duties* 3:132, pp. 88f.

85. 1 Sam 20; Cf. Spec car 3:12, 29.

was condemned to death, when he was destined for slaughter; thus Jonathan humiliated himself and exalted his friend. "You," he said, "shall be king, and I will be next after you."[86] O mirror most excellent of true friendship! Marvel of marvels! The king was enraged against his servant, and was arousing the entire country against him as one emulous of his power. Accusing the priests of treachery, he was slaying them for mere suspicion. He rages through the woods, searches the valleys, and encompasses mountains and cliffs with an armed band, while all pledge themselves vindicators of the royal wrath; Jonathan only, who alone could be somewhat justifiably envious, thought it proper to oppose his father, to defer to his friend, and to offer him counsel in the face of his opposition. Preferring friendship to a kingdom, "You," he said, "shall be king, and I will be next after you."[87] 93. And see how Saul, the father of the youth, strove to arouse envy in him against his friend, heaping him with reproaches, terrifying him with threats, reminding Jonathan that he would be despoiled of a kingdom and deprived of honor. But when Saul had uttered the sentence of death against David, Jonathan did not fail his friend. "Why shall David die? Wherein has he sinned? What has he done? He put his life in his hands, and slew the Philistine, and you rejoiced. Why, therefore, shall he die?"[88] At this utterance the king became angered and strove to nail Jonathan to the wall with his spear; and adding reproaches to threats, he said: "You son of a woman that is the ravisher of a man, I know that you love him to your own confusion and to the confusion of your shameless mother! "[89] 94. Then he spewed out poison to steep the heart of the youth, adding the word that was an inducement to ambition, a ferment of envy, an incentive to emulousness and bitterness: "As long as the son of Jesse lives, your kingdom will not be established."[90] Who would not be stirred by these words, who would not be made envious? Whose love, whose favors, whose friend-

86. 1 Sam 23:17.
87. *Ibid.*
88. 1 Sam 20:32; 19:5.
89. 1 Sam 20:30.
90. 1 Sam 20:31.

ship would these words not corrupt, nor diminish, nor obliterate? That most loving youth, preserving the laws of friendship, brave in the face of threats, patient before reproaches, despising a kingdom because of his friendship, unmindful of glory, but mindful of grace, declared: "You shall be king, and I will be next after you."[91] 95. Tullius says that some have been found who think it mean to prefer money to friendship; but that it is impossible to discover those who do not put honors, civic offices, military commands, power or riches before friendship; so that when these sentiments are offered on the one hand, and the claims of friendship on the other, they will much prefer the former. For nature is too weak to despise power.[92] "For where," he says, "will you find one who prefers the honor of his friend to his own?"[93] Behold, Jonathan was found a victor over nature, a despiser of glory and of power, one who preferred the honor of his friend to his own, saying: "You shall be king, and I will be next after you."[94] 96. This is true, perfect, constant, and eternal friendship; which envy does not corrupt, nor suspicion diminish, nor ambition dissolve; which thus tempted does not yield, thus assailed does not fall; which is perceived to be unyielding though struck by reproaches innumerable and though wounded by injuries manifold. Therefore, "go and do you in like manner."[95] But if you think it hard and even impossible to prefer him whom you love to yourself, do not fail at least to hold him on an equal footing with yourself if you wish to be a friend. 97. For they do not rightly develop friendship who do not preserve equality. "Defer to your friend as to an equal," says Ambrose, "and be not ashamed to anticipate a friend in a service. For friendship knows no pride. Indeed, a faithful friend is the medicine of live,[96] the charm of immortality."[97]

And now let us devote our attention to the question of how the benefits of friendship are to be cultivated; and on

91. 1 Sam 23:17.
92. Amic 63.
93. Amic 64.
94. 1 Sam 23:17.
95. Lk 10:37.
96. Sir 6:16.
97. *Duties* 3:128, p. 88.

this topic let us wrest some information from other's hands. "Let this law," someone says, "be established with respect to friendship, that we seek what is honorable from our friends, and ourselves perform what is honorable for them, and let us not wait to be asked. Let there never be any delay in a friend's service!"[98] 98. If we must be prepared to lose money on our friends, how much more ought we be prepared to give it to them when their advantage or their need requires it? But not all can do everything. One abounds in money, another in lands and goods; one can effect more by counsel, and still another excels in dignity of office. But in these matters consider prudently how you must conduct yourself toward your friend. And concerning money, Scripture has given ample advice: "Lose your money for your friend."[99] But as the "eyes of the wise man are in his head," let us, if we are the members and Christ the head,[100] act according to the words of the Prophet: "My eyes are ever toward the Lord";[101] so that we may receive our manner of life from the Lord, concerning which it is written: "If any want wisdom, let him ask to God, who gives to all men abundantly, and does not upbraid."[102] 99. Therefore, give to your friend in such a way that you do not reproach him, or expect a reward. Do not wrinkle your brow, or turn aside your countenance or avert your eyes; but with a serene countenance, a cheerful aspect and pleasing speech, anticipate the request of him who is seeking a favor. Meet him with kindness, so that you may appear to be granting his request without being asked.[103] The sensitive soul thinks nothing more worthy of a blush than to beg. Since, therefore, you and your friend ought to be of one heart and one soul,[104] it is unjust, if there is not also but one purse. Let this law, therefore, be held in this respect among friends, namely, that they expend themselves and their goods for one another in

98. Amic 44.
99. Sir 29:13.
100. Eph 1:22f.; 5:30; Gal 1:18.
101. Ps 24:15.
102. Jas 1:5.
103. Amic 44.
104. Acts 4:32.

such a way that he who gives preserves a cheerful aspect, and that he who receives does not lose confidence. 100. When Booz observed the poverty of Ruth, the Moabite, he spoke to her as she was gathering ears of corn behind his reapers, consoled her and invited her to the table of his servants, and sparing in kindly fashion her embarrassment, he ordered his reapers to leave ears of corn even purposely so that she might collect them without shame.[105] In the same way we ought the more adroitly seek out the needs of our friends, anticipate their requests by good services, and observe such demeanor in our giving that the recipient, rather than the giver, appears to be bestowing the favor.

Walter. But for us, who are permitted to receive nothing and to bestow nothing, what will be the charm of spiritual friendship in this respect?

101. *Aelred.* Men would lead a very happy life, says the Wise Man, if these two words were taken from their midst: namely, "mine" and "yours."[106] For holy poverty certainly bestows great strength upon spiritual friendship, poverty which is holy for the reason that it is voluntary. For since cupidity makes heavy demands on friendship, friendship once attained is the more easily preserved in proportion as the soul is found more fully purified of this pest. There are, moreover, other resources in spiritual love, by means of which friends can be of aid and advantage to one another. The first is to be solicitous for one another, to pray for one another, to blush for one another, to rejoice for one another, to grieve for one another's fall as one's own, to regard another's progress as one's own.

102. By whatever means are in one's power, one ought to raise the weak, support the infirm, console the afflicted, restrain the wrathful. Furthermore one ought so to respect the eye of a friend as to dare to do nothing which is dishonorable, or dare to say nothing which is unbecoming. For when one fails one's self in anything, the act ought so to well over to one's friend, that the sinner not only blushes and grieves

105. Ruth 2:8ff.
106. Pseudo-Seneca, *Monita,* 97.

within himself, but that even the friend who sees or hears reproaches himself as if he himself has sinned. In fact, the friend will believe that he deserves no compassion, but that his erring associate does. Therefore, the best companion of friendship is reverence, and so he who deprives friendship of respect takes away its greatest adornment.[107] 103. How often has the nod of my friend restrained or extinguished the flame of anger aroused within me and already bursting forth into public gaze! How frequently his rather severe demeanor has repressed the unbecoming word already on my lips! How often when carelessly breaking into laughter, or lapsing into idleness, I have recovered a proper dignity at his approach! Besides, whatever counsel is to be given is more easily received from a friend, and more steadfastly retained, for a friend's power in counseling must needs be great,[108] since there can neither be doubt of his loyalty nor suspicion of flattery. 104. Therefore, let friend counsel friend as to what is right, securely, openly, and freely. And friends are not only to be admonished, but if necessity arise, reproved as well. For although truth is offensive to some, seeing that hatred is born of it according to the aphorism: "Compliance begets friends, truth gives birth to hatred";[109] yet that complacency is by far more hurtful, because it indulges in wrongdoing and thus suffers a friend to be borne along headlong to ruin.[110] However, that friend is more grievously culpable and therefore especially to be reproached if he scorns truth and by complaisances and blandishments is driven to crime. Not that we ought not kindly to honor our friends and often praise them. But in all things moderation must be preserved, so that admonition be without bitterness, and reproof be without incentive. 105. Indeed, in humoring and praising let there be a certain kind and honorable friendliness; but let subserviency, the helpmate of vices, be far removed as a thing unworthy, not

107. Amic 82.
108. Amic 44.
109. Terence, *Andria,* 68; ed. J. Marouzeau, vol. 1 (Paris, 1947) p. 128; tr. P. Perry, *The Comedies of Terence* (London: Milford, 1929) p. 6.
110. Amic 89.

only of a friend, but even of any free-born person. Moreover, if a man's ears are so closed to the truth that he is not able to hear the truth from a friend, his salvation must be despaired of.[111] 106. Therefore," as Saint Ambrose says, "if you perceive any vice in your friend, correct him secretly; if he will not listen to you, correct him openly. For corrections are good and often better than a friendship which holds its peace. And even though your friend think himself wronged, nevertheless correct him. Even though the bitterness of correction wound his soul, nevertheless cease not to correct him. For the wounds inflicted by a friend are more tolerable than the kisses of flatterers.[112] Therefore, correct the erring friend."[113]

And yet, above all things, one ought to avoid anger and bitterness of spirit in correction, that he may be seen to have the betterment of his friend at heart rather than the satisfaction of his own ill humor. 107. For I have seen some, in correcting their friends, clothe with the name now of zeal, now of liberty, the bitterness within them and their outsurging rage; and because they follow impulse rather than reason, they never effect any good by such correction, but rather cause harm. But among friends there is no excuse for this vice. For a friend ought to sympathize with a friend, he ought to condescend, to think of his friend's fault as his own, to correct him humbly and sympathetically. Let a somewhat troubled countenance make the reproof, as also a saddened utterance; let tears interrupt words, so that the other may not only see but even feel that the reproof proceeds from love rather than from rancor. If he chance to have rejected the first correction, let him receive even a second. Meanwhile, pray and weep, displaying a troubled countenance, but preserving a holy affection. 108. One ought even to study the disposition of his heart. For there are those with whom coaxings are effective, and such persons quite readily assent thereto. There are others who are impervious to coaxing, and are more easily corrected by a

111. Amic 88-90.
112. Prov 27:6. Amic 91.
113. *Duties* 3:127, p. 88.

word or a blow. Let a man, therefore, conform and adapt himself to his friend to be in harmony with his disposition. As one ought to be of aid to a friend in his material setbacks, so he ought the more readily hasten to succour him in trials of the spirit. It is characteristic of friendship to admonish and to be admonished, and to do the former freely, not harshly, and to receive the latter patiently, not resentfully; so it should be understood that in friendship there is no greater pest than flattery and subserviency,[114] which are the marks of fickle and deceitful men, who speak everything at the whim of another, but speak nothing with an eye to truth. 109. Accordingly, let there be no hesitation among friends, and no pretense, a thing most of all repugnant to friendship. Indeed, a man owes truth to his friend, without which the name of friendship has no value.[115] "The just man," says holy David, "shall correct me in mercy, and shall reprove me; but let not the oil of the sinner fatten my head."[116] The pretender and the man of cunning provoke the wrath of God. Thus the Lord says through his Prophet: "O my people, they that call you blessed, the same deceive you, and destroy the way of your steps."[117] For, as Solomon says: "The dissembler with his mouth deceives his friend."[118] Therefore, friendship ought so to be cultivated that, although it may perhaps tolerate dissimulation for good reasons, it will never tolerate simulation.

Walter. How, pray, can dissimulation be necessary, a thing which, so it seems to me, is always a vice?

110. *Aelred.* You are mistaken, son, for God is said to dissimulate in regard to the sins of the delinquent,[119] not wishing the death of the sinner, but that he be converted, and live.[120]

Walter. Distinguish, please, between simulation and dissimulation.

114. Amic 91.
115. Amic 92. Cf. Bernard of Clairvaux, Ep 78:13, BLJ 80, p. 118; Ep 35, BLJ 36, p. 70.
116. Ps 145:5.
117. Is 3:12.
118. Prov 11:9.
119. Wis 11:24.
120. Ezek 33:11.

111. *Aelred.* Simulation, I think, is a kind of deceptive agreement, opposed to the judgment of reason, which Terence, in the person of Gnatho, rather excellently expressed: "Does some one say 'no'? I say 'no'. Does one say, 'yes'? I say, 'yes' too. In fine, I have ordered myself to give assent in everything."[121] Perhaps that well-known pagan borrowed these ideas from our treasures, expressing the sentiment of our Prophet in his own words. For it is clear that the Prophet said this very thing in the person of the perverted people: "See errors for us, speak unto us pleasant things."[122] And in another place: "The prophets prophesied falsehood, and the priests clapped their hands; and my people loved such things."[123] This vice should be detested everywhere, always and everywhere it should be shunned. 112. Now, dissimulation is in a sense a dispensing with, or a putting off of punishment or correction, without interior approval, in consideration of place, time, or person.[124] For if a friend when he is in the midst of others should commit some fault, he should not suddenly and publicly be reproached; but one ought to "dissemble" because of the place, nay, further, as far as is compatible with truth, one ought to excuse what he has done, and wait to administer in secret the deserved rebuke. Likewise, at a time when the mind is engrossed in many considerations and so is less receptive of those matters which must be spoken, or, when, for other reasons that have intervened, the friend's feelings are a trifle more moved and he is, in consequence, somewhat disturbed—in both instances there is need of dissimulation until the tumult within has been calmed, and he can endure without irritation the needful correction. 113. When King David, yielding to lust, added murder to adultery, the prophet Nathan was sent to correct him. Deferential to his royal majesty, he

---

121. Terence, *Eunuchus,* 252; ed. J. Marouzeau, vol. 1 (Paris, 1947) p. 239; tr. P. Perry, *The Comedies of Terence* (London: Milford, 1929) p. 140. Aelred probably received this directly from Cicero (Amic 93); however it is possible that he himself read Terence as he was widely read in the monasteries during the Middle Ages. He was frequently cited by Augustine and this would be another possible source for Aelred. Gnatho was a type of the parasitical sycophant.
122. Is 30:10.
123. Jer 5:31.
124. See Inst incl 1, CF 2:44.

did not suddenly nor with agitation of mind accuse so distinguished a personage of his crime, but using the shield of suitable dissimulation, he prudently extracted from the king himself a judgment against his own person.[125]

114. *Walter.* That distinction pleases me very much. But I should like to know whether a friend who has more power and is able to promote whomsoever he wishes to honors and distinctions, ought to prefer to others in such promotions those whom he cherishes and by whom he is cherished; and, if so, whether he ought among his friends to give precedence to those whom he loves with greater predilection?[126]

115. *Aelred.* In regard to this point it is to our advantage to examine how friendship is to be cultivated. For there are some persons who think they are not loved because they cannot be promoted, and who allege that they are despised, if they are not entrusted with responsibilities and offices. We know that as a result of this type of thinking no small discord has sprung up among those who were considered friends, so that estrangement followed upon indignation, and railings upon estrangement. Thus great caution must be observed in the conferring of dignities and offices, especially ecclesiastical ones. You should not be concerned about what you are able to bestow, but rather about what he, upon whom you bestow anything, can endure. 116. Indeed, many are to be loved, who, nevertheless, should not be advanced to office; and we happily and laudably embrace many whom we could not involve in responsibilities and undertakings without grave sin on our part and great danger on theirs. Therefore, in these matters one should always be guided by reason and not by affection. A dignity and burden of office should not be imposed on those whom we prefer as friends, but rather on those whom we believe better suited to sustain such dignities and burdens. Where, however, equality of virtue is found, I do not greatly disapprove if to some degree affection gives play to its feelings.[127]

125. 2 Sam 12:1ff.
126. Cf. Spec car 3:38.
127. Amic 73.

117. Nor should anyone say that he is held in contempt for the reasons that he is not promoted, since the Lord Jesus preferred Peter to John in this respect; nor did he, on that account, lessen his affection for John, because he had given Peter the leadership.[128] To Peter he commended his Church; to John, his most beloved Mother.[129] To Peter he gave the keys of his kingdom;[130] to John he revealed the secrets of his heart. Peter, therefore, was the more exalted;[131] John, the more secure. Although Peter was established in power, nevertheless when Jesus said, "One of you will betray me," he was afraid and trembled along with the rest; but John, leaning on the bosom of his Master, was made the bolder, and at a nod from Peter asked who the traitor was.[132] Peter, therefore, was exposed to action, John was reserved for love, according to the words of Christ: "So will I have him remain till I come."[133] Thus Christ gave us the example that we might do in like manner.[134] 118. Let us afford our friend whatever love, whatever kindness, whatever sweetness, whatever charity we can; but let us impose vain honors and burdens on those who, reason dictates, should be burdened, realizing that a man never truly loves a friend if he is not satisfied with his friend as he is, but must needs add these worthless and contemptible honors. One must also greatly guard against permitting a too tender affection from hindering greater utility.[135] This would be the case were we unwilling to part from or to burden those whom we embrace in greater charity then great hope of more abundant fruit is to be realized. For this is well-ordered friendship,

128. Cf. Conf. 16:14: "Friendship is for a few, and only for those who by identity of tastes and similarity of virtues are united to us. This is evidently referred to in what the Gospel says of St John the Evangelist, 'the disciple whom Jesus loved'; since he certainly loved with a special affection the other eleven who had been chosen by him. . . ." Cf. Spec car 3:39.—SCh 54:233-234, CS 31.

129. Jn 19:26f.
130. Mt 16:19.
131. Cf. Inst incl 31, CF 2:87.
132. Jn 13:21ff.
133. Jn 21:22.
134. Jn 13:15.
135. Amic 79.

namely, that reason rules affection, and that we attend more to the general welfare than to our friend's good humor.[136]

119. I recall now two friends, who, although they have passed from this present life, nevertheless live to me and always will so live.[137] The first of these I gained as my friend when I was still young, in the beginning of my conversion, because of a certain resemblance between us in character and similarity of interests;[138] the other I chose when he was still a boy, and after I had tested him repeatedly in various ways, when at length age was silvering my hair, I admitted him into my most intimate friendship.[139] Indeed, I chose the former as my companion, as the one who shared in the delights of the cloister and the spiritual joys which I was just beginning to taste when I, too, was not as yet burdened with any pastoral duty or perplexed with temporal affairs. I demanded nothing and I bestowed nothing but affection and the loving judgment of affection itself according as charity dictated. The latter I claimed when he was still young to be a sharer in my anxieties and a co-worker in these labors of mine. Looking back, as far as my memory permits, upon each of these friendships, I see that the first rested for the most part on affection and the second on reason, although affection was not lacking in the latter, or reason in the former. 120. In fine, my first friend, taken from me in the very beginnings of our friendship, I was

136. Cf. Spec car 3:18: "For this is rightly ordered affection: not to love what is not to be loved; to love what is to be loved; but not to love in a greater measure than what is due; not to love with equal affection those things which should be loved in different degrees; not to love in different measure those things that should be equally loved." Cf. Bernard of Clairvaux, Ep 85:3, BLJ 87, p. 162: ". . . that I may see and rejoice at the rightly ordered charity in me, knowing and loving what ought to be loved, as much as they should be loved, and for the reason that they should be loved; being unwilling also to be loved except in you, and only in so far as I should be loved."

137. Amic 102.

138. Cf. *Confessions* 4:4. This first friend is usually identified as Aelred's beloved Simon whose death wrung from him the very heartfelt lament which we find in Spec car 1:34.

139. Powicke identifies this second friend as being Geoffrey of Dinant whom Aelred brought back to Rievaulx when he returned from Rome in 1142; see F. M. Powicke, *Aelred of Rievaulx and his Biographer Walter Daniel* (Manchester: Longmans Green and Co., 1922) p. 50; see also Dubois, *L'amitié*, p. lxxxviii.

able to choose, as I have said, but not to test; the other, devoted to me from boyhood even to middle age, and loved by me, mounted with me through all the stages of friendship, as far as human imperfection permitted. And, indeed, it was my admiration for his virtues that first directed my affection toward him, and it was I who long ago brought him from the South to this northern solitude, and first introduced him to regular discipline. From that time he learned to conquer his own flesh and to endure labor and hunger;[140] to very many he was an example, to many a source of admiration, and to myself a source of honor and delight. Already at that time I thought that he should be nurtured in the beginnings of friendship, seeing that he was a burden to no one but pleasing to all. 121. He came and went, hastening at the command of his superiors, humble, gentle, reserved in manner, sparing of speech, a stranger to indignation, and unacquainted with murmuring, rancor, and detraction; he walked "as one deaf, hearing not, and as one dumb, not opening his mouth."[141] "He became as a beast of burden,"[142] submissive to the reins of obedience, and bearing untiringly the yoke of regular discipline in mind and body. Once when he was still young he was in the infirmary and he was rebuked by my holy father and predecessor[143] for yielding so early in life to rest and inactivity. The boy was so ashamed at this that he immediately left the infirmary and subjected himself with such zeal to corporal labor that for many years he would not allow himself any relaxation from his accustomed rigor, even when he was afflicted with serious illness.[144] 122. All this in a most wondrous way had bound him to me by the most intimate bonds, and had so brought him into my affection, that from an inferior I made him my companion, from a companion a friend, from a friend my most cherished of friends.[145] For when I saw that he had advanced far in the life of virtue and grace,

140. Cf. Sallust, *Catilina*, 5:3; Watson, p. 10.
141. Ps 37:14.
142. Ps 72:22.
143. Abbot Maurice who had resigned as Abbot of Rievaulx in 1147.
144. Cf. *Confessions* 7:21.
145. Cf. Spec car 129.

I consulted the brethren and imposed upon him the burden of subpriorship. This burden, against his will, to be sure, but because he had vowed himself to obedience, he modestly accepted. Yet he pleaded with me in secret to be relieved of it, alleging as excuse his age, his lack of knowledge, and finally the friendship which we had but lately formed, fearful that this might prove to be an occasion for him either to love the less or to be loved the less.[146] 123. But, availing nothing by these entreaties, then he began to reveal quite freely but at the same time humbly and modestly what he feared for each of us, and what in me pleased him but little. He hoped thereby, as he afterwards confessed, that I would be offended by this presumption, and would the more easily be inclined to grant his request. But his freedom of speech and spirit only led our friendship to its culmination, for my desire for his friendship was lessened not a whit. Perceiving then that his words had pleased me, and that I answered humbly to each accusation and had satisfied him in all these matters, and that he himself had not only caused no offense but rather had received more fruitful benefit, he began to manifest his love for me even more ardently than theretofore, to relax the reins of his affection,[147] and to reveal himself wholly to my heart. In this way we tested one another, I making proof of his freedom of utterance and he of my patience. 124. And I, too, repaid my friend in kind in his turn. Thinking that I should at an opportune moment harshly reprove him, I did not spare him any, as it were, reproaches, and I found him patient with my frankness and grateful. Then I began to reveal to him the secrets of my innermost thoughts, and I found him faithful. In this way love increased between us, affection glowed the warmer and charity was strengthened, until we attained that stage at which we had but one mind and one soul[148] to will and not to will alike,[149] and at which our love was devoid of fear and ignorant of offense, shunning suspicion and abhorring flat-

146. Cf. Bernard of Clairvaux, Ep 85, BLJ 87, pp. 125ff.
147. Amic 45.
148. Acts 4:32.
149. See above, 1:40, n. 35.

tery. 125. There was no pretense between us, no simulation, no dishonorable flattery, no unbecoming harshness, no evasion, no concealment, but everything open and above board; for I deemed my heart in a fashion his, and his mine, and he felt in like manner towards me. And so, as we were progressing in friendship without deviation, neither's correction evoked the indignation of the other, neither's yielding produced blame. Therefore, proving himself a friend in every respect, he provided as much as was in his power for my peace and my rest. He exposed himself to dangers and he forestalled scandals in their very inception. 126. Occasionally I wanted to provide him for his ailments with some alleviation from creature comforts, but he opposed it, saying that we should be on our guard against having our love measured according to the consolation of the flesh, and of having the gift be ascribed to my carnal affection rather than to his need, with the resultant effect that my authority might in consequence be diminished. He was, therefore, as it were, my hand, my eye,[150] the staff of my old age.[151] He was the refuge of my spirit, the sweet solace of my griefs, whose heart of love received me when fatigued from labors, whose counsel refreshed me when plunged in sadness and grief. 127. He himself calmed me when distressed, he soothed me when angry. Whenever anything unpleasant occurred, I referred it to him, so that, shoulder to shoulder, I was able to bear more easily what I could not bear alone. What more is there, then, that I can say? Was it not a foretaste of blessedness thus to love and thus to be loved;[152] thus to help and thus to be helped; and in this way from the sweetness of fraternal charity to wing one's flight aloft to that more sublime splendor of divine love, and by the ladder of charity now to mount to the embrace of Christ himself; and again to descend to the love of neighbor, there pleasantly to rest? And so, in this friendship of ours, which we have introduced by way of example, if you see aught worthy of imitation, profit by it to advance your own perfection.

150. A common image coming from antiquity. It is found already in Xenophon, *Memorables*, 2:4.

151. Tob 5:23.

152. See above, Prologue, note 1, p. 45.

128. But since it is growing late and we must at last close this discussion of ours, you are surely convinced that friendship is founded on love. Indeed, who is there that can love another, if he does not love himself since, from a comparison with that love by which he is dear to himself, a man ought to regulate his love for his neighbor. A man does not love himself who exacts of himself or commands from himself anything shameful or dishonorable. 129. In the first place, then, one must needs chastize one's self, allowing nothing which is unbecoming and refusing nothing which is profitable. And loving himself thus, let him follow the same rule in loving his neighbor.[153] But as this love includes many persons, let him choose from among them one whom he can admit in familiar fashion to the mysteries of friendship, and upon whom he can bestow his affection in abundance, laying bare his mind and heart even to their sinews and marrow, that is, even to the most secret thoughts and desires of the heart. 130. Let such a friend be chosen, moreover, not according to the caprice of affection but rather according to the foresight of reason, because of similarity of character and the contemplation of virtue. Then let a man so attach himself to his friend that all levity be absent and all joy be present, and let there be no lack of proper services and courtesies of benevolence and charity.

Next let the loyalty of your proposed friend be tested, as well as his honor and his patience. Let there gradually be added sharing of counsels, application to common concern and a certain conformity in outward expression. 131. For friends ought to be so alike that immediately upon seeing one another a likeness of expression is reflected from the first to the second, whether he be cast down by sorrow or serene with joy. After he has thus been chosen and tested, and when you are assured that he will wish to ask of a friend or to do himself if asked nothing that would be unbecoming; and moreover, when you are confident that he looks upon friendship as a

---

153. Cf. Augustine, *Soliloquies,* 1:8; tr. C. Starbuck in *Basic Writings of Saint Augustine,* vol. 1 (New York: Random House, 1948) p. 263.

virtue and not as a trade, and that he shuns flattery and detests
obsequiousness; and finally, when you have discovered that
he is frank, yet with discretion, patient under reproof, firm
and constant in affection, then you will experience that spiritual delight, namely, "how good and how pleasant it is for
brethren to dwell together in unity."[154] 132. How advantageous
it is then to grieve for one another, to toil for one another, to
bear one another's burdens,[155] while each considers it sweet
to forget himself for the sake of the other, to prefer the will
of the other to his own, to minister to the other's needs rather
than one's own, to oppose and expose one's self to misfortunes! Meanwhile, how delightful friends find it to converse
with one another, mutually to reveal their interests, to examine all things together, and to agree on all of them! 133.
Added to this there is prayer for one another,[156] which, coming from a friend, is the more efficacious in proportion as it is
more lovingly sent to God, with tears which either fear excites or affection awakens or sorrow evokes. And thus a friend
praying to Christ on behalf of his friend, and for his friend's
sake desiring to be heard by Christ, directs his attention with
love and longing to Christ; then it sometimes happens that
quickly and imperceptibly the one love passes over into the
other, and coming, as it were, into close contact with the
sweetness of Christ himself, the friend begins to taste his
sweetness and to experience his charm.[157] 134. Thus ascending
from that holy love with which he embraces a friend to that
with which he embraces Christ, he will joyfully partake in
abundance of the spiritual fruit of friendship, awaiting the
fullness of all things in the life to come. Then, with the dispel-
ling of all anxiety by reason of which we now fear and are
solicitous for one another, with the removal of all adversity
which it now behooves us to bear for one another, and, above
all, with the destruction of the sting of death together with

154. Ps 132:1.
155. Gal 6:2.
156. See above, n. 101. Cf. Augustine, Ep 145:7; 186:41; 20:2.
157. Ps 33:9; 99:5. Cf. Oner 3, PL 195:371A; CF 26; Iesu 1:8, CF 2:12; Walter
Daniel, *Centum Sententiae*, 79, *loc. cit.*, pp. 344ff.

death itself,[158] whose pangs now often trouble us and force us to grieve for one another, with salvation secured, we shall rejoice in the eternal possession of Supreme Goodness; and this friendship, to which here we admit but few, will be out-poured upon all and by all outpoured upon God, and God shall be all in all.[159]

158. 1 Cor 15:54f.
159. 1 Cor 15:28.

ABBREVIATIONS

Amic
    Marcus Tullius Cicero, *On Friendship*, Tr. W. Falconer in *De Senectute—De Amicitia—De Divinatione* (New York: Putnam, 1922) pp. 108-211.

BLJ
    Bernard of Clairvaux, *Letters.* Tr. B. S. James, *The Letters of St Bernard of Clairvaux* (London: Burns Oates, 1953).

CC
    Corpus christianorum, series Latina (Turnhout: Brepols, 1945—).

CCM
    Corpus christianorum continuatio mediaevalis (Turnhout: Brepols, 1971—).

CF
    Cistercian Fathers Series (Spencer, Mass., Washington, D. C.: Cistercian Publications, 1970—).

Conf.
    John Cassian, *Conferences,* SCh 42, 54, 64 (1955, 1958, 1959). Tr. G. Scannell, CS 20, 31.

Confessions Augustine of Hippo, *Confessions.* Tr. J. G. Pilkington in *Basic Writings of Saint Augustine* (New York: Random House, 1948) 1:3-256.

CS
    Cistercian Studies Series (Spencer, Mass., Washington, D. C.: Cistercian Publications, 1969—).

Duties Ambrose of Milan, *Duties of the Clergy*. Tr. H. de Romestin in *Nicene and Post-Nicene Fathers,* series 2 (Grand Rapids: Eerdmans, 1955) 10:1-89.

Ep Letter(s).

Friends A. M. Fiske, *Friends and Friendship in the Monastic Tradition,* Cidoc Cuaderno 51 (Cuernavaca: CIDOC, 1970).

Iesu Aelred of Rievaulx, *Jesus at the Age of Twelve,* CCM 1:249-278. Tr. Theodore Berkeley in *The Works of Aelred of Rievaulx,* CF 2:41-102.

Inst inclu Aelred of Rievaulx, *A Rule of Life for a Recluse,* CCM 1:637-682. Tr. M. P. Macpherson in *The Works of Aelred of Rievaulx,* CF 2:41-102.

Life Walter Daniel, *The Life of Ailred of Rievaulx.* Ed. and tr. F. M. Powicke (London: Nelson, 1950).

Monastic
Order David Knowles, *The Monastic Order in England,* 2nd ed. (Cambridge University, 1963).

OB *Sancti Bernardi opera.* Ed. J. Leclercq, C. H. Talbot, H. M. Rochais (Rome: Editiones Cistercienses, 1957–).

Oner Aelred of Rievaulx, *Sermons on Isaiah.* PL 195: 363-500; CS 26.

PL *Patrologiae cursus completus, series Latina* Ed. J.P. Migne (Paris, 1878-1890).

RB *St. Benedict's Rule for Monasteries,* SCh 181, 182. Ed. Adalbert de Vogüé (1972). Tr. Leonard Doyle (Collegeville: Liturgical Press, 1948).

SC   Bernard of Clairvaux, *Sermons on the Song of Songs.* OB 1 and 2. Tr. Kilian Walsh in *The Works of Bernard of Clairvaux*, CF4, 7, 31, 40.

SCh   Sources chrétiennes (Paris: Cerf, 1943—).

Spec car   Aelred of Rievaulx, *The Mirror of Charity*, CCM 1:3-161. Tr. Pierre Fortin in *The Works of Aelred of Rievaulx*, CF 17.

Spir amic   Aelred of Rievaulx, *Spiritual Friendship*, CCM 1:287-350. Tr. E. Laker in *The Works of Aelred of Rievaulx*, CF 5.

SELECTED BIBLIOGRAPHY

Sources

Aelred of Rievaulx (St), *Spiritual Friendship:*
  Dubois, J., ed., *L'amitié spirituelle,* Latin text, translation, notes (Bruges: C. Beyaert, 1948).
Hoste, A., ed., *De Spiritali Amicitia,* critical edition, CCM 1:287-350
  Magna Bibliotheca Veterum Patrum (Cologne, 1618) vol. 13, pp. 129-143.
  Maxima Bibliotheca Veterum Patrum (Lyons, 1677) vol. 33, pp. 138-153.
Migne, J.P., ed., *Beati Aelredi Abbatis Rievallensis Opera Omnia* (Paris, 1855) PL 195:659-702.
Tissier, B., ed., *Bibliotheca Patrum Cisterciensium* (Bonnefontaine,1662) vol. 5, pp. 362-380.
Ambrose of Milan (St) *De Officiis Ministrorum,* ed., J.P. Migne (Paris, 1845) PL 16:28-184.
Cassian, J., *Conferences,* ed., E. Pichery, *Conferences,* 3 vols, SCh 42, 54,64 (Paris: Cerf, 1955-1959), Conference 16: *De Amicitia,* 2:221 - 247.
Cicero, Marcus Tullius, *De Senectute—De Amicitia—De Divinatione,* Latin text, translation, W. Falconer (New York: Putnam, 1922).
Daniel, Walter, *The Life of Ailred of Rievaulx,* ed., F. M. Powicke (London: Nelson, 1950).

Translations

Delfendahl, B., "On Human Friendship" in *The Life of the Spirit,* 8 (1953) pp. 119-128. (extracts)
Ingham, F., *Aelred de Rievaulx: Traité de l'amitié spirituelle* (Brussels: Cité Chrétienne, 1938).
Jerome, Sr. M. F., *Of Spiritual Friendship* (Paterson, N.J.: St Anthony's Guild, 1948).
Otten, K., *Die heilige Freundschaft* (Munich, 1927).

137

Talbot, H., *Christian Friendship* (London: Catholic Book Club, 1942).
Vanderspeeten, S., *Lois et douceurs de l'amitié spirituelle* (Brussels, 1885).

Studies

(anonymous) *Saint Aelred, abbé de Rievaulx, sa vie et ses oeuvres.* Lérins, 1878.
Bouyer, Louis, *The Cistercian Heritage*, tr. E. Livingston. Westminster, Md.: Newman, 1958.
Brodrick, J., "St. Aelred, Abbot of Rievaulx" in *The Clergy Review*, 26 (1946) pp. 27-36.
Burridge, A., "The Spirituality of St. Aelred" in *Downside Review*, 58 (1940) pp. 225-247.
Chenevière, E., *Nos Pères par euxmêmes*, ms., vol. 1. pp. 101-161.
Courcelle, P., "Ailred de Rievaulx à l'école des *Confessions*" in *Revue des études augustiniennes*, 3 (1957) pp. 163-174.
Delhave, P., "Deux adaptations du 'De Amicita' de Cicéron au XIIe siècle" in *Recherches de théologie ancienne et médiévale*, 15 (1948) pp. 304-331.
Ducey, W. M., "St. Ailred of Rievaulx and the *Speculum Caritatis*" in *Catholic Historical Review*, 17 (1931) pp. 308-317.
Dumont, C., "Aelred de Rievaulx" in *Théologie de la vie monastique* Paris: Aubier, 1961, pp. 527-538.
—— "St Aelred: The Balanced Life of the Monk" in *Monastic Studies*, 1 (1963), pp. 25-58.
Fiske, A., *Friends and Friendship in the Monastic Tradition*, Cidoc Cuaderno 51. Cuernavaca: CIDOC, 1970.
Gilson, E., *The Mystical Theology of Saint Bernard*, tr. A. Downes. New York: Sheed and Ward, 1940.
Hallier, A., *The Monastic Theology of Aelred of Rievaulx: An Experiential Theology*, CS 2. Spencer, Mass.: Cistercian Publications, 1969.
Harvey, T. E., *Saint Aelred of Rievaulx*. London, 1932.
Haskins, C. H. *The Renaissance of the Twelfth Century*. Cambridge: Harvard University Press, 1927.
Hoste, A., *Bibliotheca Aelrediana*. Steenbrugge: Sint Petersabdij, 1962. 1962).
—— "Le traité psuedo-augustinien De Amicitia: un résumé d'un ouvrage authentique d'Aelred de Rievaulx" in *Revue des études augustiniennes*, 6 (1960) pp. 155-159.
—— "Marginalia bij Aelred's *De institutione inclusarum*" in *Cîteaux in de Nederlanden*, 9 (1958) pp. 132-136.
Hunt, W., "Ethelred" in *Dictionary of National Biography*, 6 (1908), pp. 897f.

Jarret, B., "Aelred" in *The English Way*, ed., M. Ward. New York: Sheed and Ward, 1933, pp. 81-103.

Le Bail, A., "Aelred" in *Dictionnaire de spiritualité*, 1 (1937) cols. 225-234.

—— "L'influence de Saint Bernard sur les auteurs spirituels de son temps" in *Saint Bernard et son temps*. Dijon: Association Bourguegnonne des Sociétés Savantes, 1928, vol. 1, pp. 205-215.

—— "La spiritualité cistercienne" in *Cahier du cercle thomiste*. Paris, 1927.

Lepp, I., *The Ways of Friendship*, trans. B. Murchland. New York: Macmillan. 1966.

McNamara, Sr. M. A., *Friends and Friendship for Saint Augustine*. Staten Island: Alba House, 1964.

Newman, J. H., *Lives of the English Saints*, ed. J. B. Dailgairns. London: Freemantle and Picadilly, 1903, vol. 5, pp. 55-428.

Pedrick, B., "Some Reflections on St. Aelred of Rievaulx" in *Buckfast Abbey Chronicle*, 14 (1944) pp. 10-25.

Powicke, F. M. *Ailred of Rievaulx and his Biographer Walter Daniel*. Manchester: Longmans Green & Co, 1922.

Raciti, Gaetano, "L'apport original d'Aelred de Rievaulx à la réflexion occidentale sur l'amitié" in *Collectanea Cisterciensia*, 29 (1967) pp. 77-99.

Schilling, R., "Aelredus von Rievaulx: *Deus Amicitia est*" in *Cîteaux in de Nederlanden*, 8 (1957) pp. 13-26.

Squire, A., *Aelred of Rievaulx: A Study*. London: SPCK, 1969.

—— "Aelred of Rievaulx and the Monastic Tradition concerning Action and Contemplation" in *Downside Review*, 72 (1954) pp. 289-303.

Vansteenberghe, G., "Amitié" in *Dictionnaire de spiritualité*, vol. 1 (1937) cols. 500-529.

—— "Deux théoriciens de l'amitié au XIIᵉ siècle: Pierre de Blois et Aelred de Riéval" in *Revue des sciences religieuses*, 12 (1932) pp. 572-588.

Watkin, A., "Saint Aelred of Rievaulx" in *The Month*, 21 (1959) pp. 273-283.

ANALYTIC INDEX

The first number refers to the book; the number(s) after the colon refer to the sections within the book.

141

TITLES LISTING

THE CISTERCIAN FATHERS SERIES

THE CISTERCIAN STUDIES SERIES

Temporarily out of print † *Forthcoming*